Never Too Late

To You.

You are beautiful.
Totally perfect. Yet still,
You seek to improve.

Never Too Late

Get Unstuck, Escape Mediocrity, and Design a Life You Love

Mike Herzog

Someritus LLC

PO Box 54, Lafayette, Indiana, 47902

Copyright © 2019 By Mike Herzog

First Printing

Published in the United States

By Someritus LLC

ISBN: 978-1-7340620-0-7:

Developmental Editing by Robyn Passante
Cover Design by BuzBooks

Contents

◆ ◆ ◆

BOOK THREE - THE REWARD

Warning

◆◆◆

It's time for honesty. Time for a little tough love.

If you purchased this book hoping to find a simple solution to the problems in your life, you may want to reconsider. Within these pages you'll find no easy answers or quick fixes. No foolproof systems. There's no miracle technology that will change everything with the push of a button. There's no magic lamp. No genie.

Books like this usually make big promises and then fail to deliver on them. Why is that? Why is this book different? I've thought about these questions a lot.

As a professional coach and organizational consultant, I've spent the past 25 years helping thousands of individuals and organizations create and sustain profound change. I've had the honor and privilege to study under some great masters. I've read countless books, attended dozens of weekend seminars, watched a lifetime of YouTube videos, and followed my fair share of charismatic gurus promising answers.

Here's what I've noticed...

They all make the same promise. Some of them do it explicitly and some of them do it on the sly. Slick and subtle. But they all do it.

They promise it will be easy.

Just change X, and you'll get Y. Guaranteed. Just follow this simple formula and you will win the game.

The prospect is enticing, isn't it? Unfortunately, quick-acting usually isn't long-lasting.

When it comes to creating a meaningful life, it's never easy and you should be suspicious of anyone who tells you otherwise.

Never Too Late is not about solutions. It's about changing the way you think about the challenges in your life. It's about changing the way you think about your place in this world. It's about developing the habits, skills, and capacities that will allow you to handle **ANY** situation that life throws your way.

Never Too Late is a process. It's a demanding one, at that. If you are not ready to put in some effort, if you're not willing to work up a sweat, walk away now.

This book isn't a solution.

It's an invitation.

Introduction: A Quest for Vision

◆◆◆

I plunged my foot into the frigid water. The creek was a threshold, both metaphorically and literally. A gateway into the Gila National Forest, where I would spend the next five days.

I had no food. Not because I was planning to live off the land, but because I wouldn't be eating. I had very little equipment. Just my sleeping bag and a bright blue plastic tarp. Comfort wasn't part of the plan, either. I had forsaken all of the modern tools that we rely on each day to distract us from reality. No phone. No music. Not even a book to read. Just a single spiral notebook and my trusty pen.

Was I insane? No. Well, not really.

I was about to embark upon a vision quest.

The vision quest is a tradition that spans generations, geography, and culture. Every spiritual leader from the Buddha, to Moses, to Christ, to Mohammed, is said to have experienced a form of vision quest. I was in pretty good company.

The vision quest typically consists of three primary elements.

Fasting. (a.k.a. "hunger.")

Check.

Nature. (a.k.a. "danger.")

Check.

Solitude. (a.k.a. "boredom.")

Check.

In the Native American culture, the vision quest was a right-of-passage that marked the transition from childhood to adulthood and usually resulted in the individual receiving a new tribal name.

I wasn't seeking a new name. I was perfectly happy with the one I already had. I was definitely seeking *something*, though I didn't know what.

I can say for certain that my own mortality weighed heavily on my mind. Just five days earlier I had lost my father after a gratefully short battle with Alzheimer's. And one year prior to that, almost to the day, my beloved coach and mentor, James, died at the age of 44, while doing his own vision quest.

The thought that I might not return across that threshold definitely crossed my mind. I wasn't seeking death, but I wanted to understand it.

I was also at a crossroads in my professional life. After what felt like a long and successful career in consulting, I was beginning to wonder what many people in their 40s wonder...does this ladder lead anywhere? I was starting to think the answer was *no*.

I found myself fairly content and comfortable in my life while simultaneously, oddly, discontent and uncomfortable. Part of me knew there was something else that I should be doing. That I *needed* to be doing. Part of me knew what *it* was. There was one problem. I was terrified to name it, let alone do it.

In the end, I guess that's what my vision quest was all about — having a conversation with the parts of me that longed to do something different with my life, and the parts of me that wanted to keep me safe and sound in the cocoon of my current existence.

Years later, I recognize my vision quest as something I call a **designed disturbance**. And disturb me it did. I have never been the same since.

Somehow, I survived my five days in the Gila wilderness. Without pizza and without Starbucks. Over the course of those five days I had many insights and epiphanies. I had a few encounters with nature, most of which led directly to the insights and epiphanies.

I said goodbye to my father.

I said hello to my new self.

And I got a new name.

My life fundamentally changed after my week in the wilderness, though I wouldn't say the vision quest caused the change. I was already standing at the threshold of change. I needed the motivation to cross that threshold.

I needed something to disturb my system.

I hope this book serves as a disturbance for yours.

How to Read this Book

◆ ◆ ◆

This book is meant to be a sprint through the woods. Fast and furious. It's designed to get your heart pounding and your mind racing with possibilities and potential. I recommend you go all-out the first time through. Get to the end as quickly as you can.

But when you sprint through the woods, you're likely to not soak in everything around you. You only experience a blur of the vibrant colors, a faint whiff of the subtle smells, and a momentary glimpse at the life teeming around you. You miss most of the experience.

So, after the first pass, I recommend you go back and read it again, slower and more deliberately. Take some time to look around. Stop, every once in a while, and examine something that you missed the first time. You'll be amazed at how much there is, right in front of you.

To assist you with that deeper exploration, we've provided a Digital Appendix that accompanies this book. There you will find downloadable worksheets that correspond to the chapters and exercises. You'll also find a number of assessments and tools designed to help you further your understanding of the concepts and to increase your self-awareness.

You can access the Digital Appendix here:
www.nevertoolatebook.com

BOOK ONE

—

The Challenge

The Pebble Problem

◆◆◆

Have you ever had a pebble in your shoe, but rather than stop and take off your shoe to shake the stone out, you decide to work around it? You desperately try to coax the pebble to the outside where it won't be as bothersome. You scrunch, you shake, you may even walk on your tiptoes for a few steps. Anything to make it less annoying. Finally, you get the pebble to the edge of your shoe, where you barely notice it. A feeling of satisfaction washes over you. *Victory!* Until a few steps later when the pebble slips back underfoot.

Most of us are walking through life with a pebble in our shoe. We tell ourselves it's not that bad. We convince ourselves things will get better. We spend all of our energy trying to get it to the point where we can tolerate having the pebble in our shoe.

Why don't we just take off our shoe and shake the damn thing out?

The Nail Problem

◆◆◆

Is it really just a pebble?

Some of us are walking through life with an honest-to-God nail coming up through the bottom of our shoe and we have no idea how to get it out. Or worse, we've managed to convince ourselves the nail is just a pebble.

Life By Default

◆ ◆ ◆

"Default" (noun)

A. (A): a selection made usually automatically or without active consideration due to lack of a viable alternative
B. (B) : (computers) a selection automatically used by a program in the absence of a choice made by the user

From www.merriam-webster.com (2019)

What is the default position when it comes to our lives?

It's passively accepting the way things are right now. It's living in a way that doesn't require any extra effort, or really even much thought. It's taking the path of least resistance rather than taking the path we'd prefer. It's living with the pebble in our shoe.

Take a moment to examine your current reality.

What is your default behavior when you come home from work? Do you flop down in front of the television or scroll mindlessly on your smartphone? What is your default way of interacting with your significant other? Do you have a set of habitual routines that keep you operating from a safe distance all the time? What is your default with regards to your physical health? Do you default to movement? To ice cream? To negative self-talk while eating ice cream?

We've all been there.

Living by default becomes an addiction. It starts off as a

pebble in our shoe. No big deal. But eventually we start allowing the default to rule bigger and bigger parts of our life. A crummy career? I can live with that. A relationship that absolutely sucks the life out of me? I can live with that. A soul that hasn't stirred in decades?

You get the picture.

Life is perfectly willing to offer us the default position and we gladly accept it because the default position is easy. The default position is familiar. The default position doesn't require us to change anything. Default never demands that we ask ourselves difficult questions. It's a good thing, because that might cause us to become uncomfortably aware, or cause us to question ourselves, to really examine our desires, motivations and our potential. *That sounds like a lot of hard work. Maybe I'll just keep going with the flow…*

Don't do it. Do not accept the default position in any aspect of your life. Accepting the default leads to mediocrity, and life is simply too short to tolerate mediocrity.

Don't choose **Life By Default**.

Default Living is "Good Enough"

◆◆◆

It's time for a riddle.

When does a positive plus a positive equal a negative?

Answer: The phrase "Good Enough."

By themselves, "good" and "enough" are two perfectly pleasant words. They're polite. They never get into trouble. But when you put the two of them together … well, you get nothing but trouble.

The biggest problem with Life By Default is that it's "good enough."

Default Living Makes You a Victim

◆ ◆ ◆

Life By Default often requires us to play the role of a victim. We convince ourselves of our misfortune and we tell ourselves we have no other choice. We blame the circumstances. We do this because accepting the role of the victim is easy and it explains absolutely everything. It relieves us of all obligations. It's not our job to make things better.

What makes someone a victim?

I used to think it was when something happens to someone that is both bad and beyond control. Then I met Nick Vujicic. Nick was born with no arms and no legs. Take a moment to process that. He was born with no arms and no legs. Now let me ask you … how big are your challenges?

Here's the crazy thing. Nick is one of the happiest, most optimistic people I've ever encountered. I thought it was an act, until I met him. It's no act. Nobody can act that well.

This guy has as much right to play the victim card as anyone, yet he never does. It's actually kind of annoying. I listened to Nick telling his story and I tried to find holes. I tried to convince myself that Nick didn't have it so bad. I needed to make myself feel better … not about Nick, but about me. I bet lots of other people have a similar reaction when they meet Nick. It's the only way our victimhood makes sense when it comes face to face with Nick's optimism.

How can I possibly be a victim if this guy isn't?

Back to the original question: What does it take to be a victim? Two things, I think.

First, we feel disempowered. We've all experienced the feeling that we have no control, no way to influence a situation. It's the worst feeling.

Second, we blame external factors. It might be another person or a group of people. We might blame some inanimate force of nature. Maybe we blame God. We might just chalk it up to bad luck. Whatever it is, it isn't us. It didn't come from within the locus of our control.

To be a victim, we must feel disempowered AND we must blame some outside force for it.

Perhaps this is how you feel right now about some aspect of your life. You probably have good reasons.

And then there's Nick Vujicic.

Default Living Debilitates

◆◆◆

You may still be wondering, *What's the big deal about default?* You may think Life By Default doesn't sound that bad. *A pebble in my shoe? Pebbles are tiny! I can live with that.* Besides, you don't feel like a victim, so no worries there. Plus, Life By Default sounds pretty easy. Come to think of it, your life is probably good enough.

There's something I didn't mention about Life By Default. It has an even darker side. Default is incredibly patient and does its damage slowly over time.

The next five chapters detail the most insidious ways that Life By Default destroys your body, erodes your relationships, stunts your growth, kills your creativity, and suppresses your soul.

Default Living
Destroys Your Body

◆◆◆

I want you to try an experiment. I'll give you 20 bucks if, for one week, you stop brushing your teeth. Just one week.

Ewww. You would never do this, right? Why not? Aside from horrific halitosis, the consequences are relatively limited. As long as you started brushing again when the week was over, your teeth (and breath) would be okay. You'd survive.

The importance of regularly brushing our teeth is something that's been ingrained in our psyches since early childhood and we've adopted this as a beneficial, long-term behavior. Yet when it comes to other areas of our health and well-being, we often make decisions that favor the short-term at the expense the long-term. I'm talking about our eating and drinking habits. Our relationship with exercise and with sleep. I'm talking about how we manage stress.

We often opt for pleasure and enjoyment right here, right now, even if there are subtle, long-term, negative consequences. We default to the now.

Living entirely in the short-term is addictive. What starts as a cheat-meal becomes a cheat-day. Eventually you've got a full-blown cheat-month on your hands. Little by little, it becomes our default way of operating. Unfortunately, the consequences of this Life By Default behavior probably won't manifest for a long time and when they do, it will be sudden — and likely catastrophic.

Here's the inevitable truth and we all know it … if we are struggling with our health, we will struggle in every other aspect of life. It's that simple. Everything starts with physical well-being. When our body is strong, we have the energy to take on challenges and to keep up with life's long haul.

Life By Default takes that away.

Default Living
Erodes Relationships

◆◆◆

What is the most important factor when it comes to our overall happiness? There's a lot of evidence to support the idea that it's the quality of our relationships. What good is having a huge pile of money if you can't share your experiences with someone else? What good is being super-healthy if you feel all alone? Relationships and connection are at the core of everything.

Of course, relationships and connection require work. Let's face it, most people are confusing as hell. Everyone is unique and even the healthiest, most open relationships require ongoing maintenance. Romantic relationships require even more attention and energy to keep things interesting and rewarding. Developing deep friendships takes time and requires emotional investment. Developing strong professional relationships and networks requires lots of energy and demands that we accommodate a raft of different styles and personalities. These things are incompatible with Life By Default.

Life By Default is all about avoiding work and effort. It's about avoiding situations where we are uncomfortable and vulnerable. Life By Default doesn't encourage us to make new connections or to deepen existing ones. It doesn't inspire us to address problems when they arise. Life By Default tells us to stay away and to ignore the issue. Don't make waves. Avoid conflict at all cost.

Life By Default erodes relationships from the outside and from the inside.

Default Living
Stunts Your Growth

◆◆◆

When did you stop growing?

I'm not talking height. I'm talking about personal growth. Learning. Developing new skills and emotional capacities. When did that stop? When you got out of school? After you got your first job? When you moved out of your parents' house?

I hope you haven't stopped growing and you don't ever plan to stop.

Default thinking tells us that stopping is allowed. Default thinking tells us that stopping is desirable. The default feels easy and we know that growth requires effort. It requires being lost from time to time so that we can emerge from the wilderness stronger and wiser.

Development sounds hard. It sounds scary. It's so much easier to sit back and just enjoy the things we're already good at. It's easier to stay in our comfort zone.

I started playing lacrosse in high school. I wasn't the biggest guy on the field, but I had decent stick handling ... with my right hand, that is. I never wanted to work on my left hand. I was able to get by. My right-hand-only technique was good enough. In high school, it was fine. But when I got to college, where the competition stiffened, my weakness was exposed. Defenders quickly realized I couldn't go left so they forced me to do exactly that. It was a real struggle and it made me wish I'd invested more time being uncomfortable when I was in high school. It made me regret that I chose to stop growing.

When we decide to stop growing, it feels fine in the moment. We probably won't feel the negative consequences for a long time. The problem is that when we stop growing, we're not able to adapt to increasingly complex situations. It may be awhile before that complexity shows up in our life, but it will. By then, it will be too late. We'll be trapped in our current self with our limited capacity. We'll blame the circumstances when we really should be blaming ourselves for making the decision to stop growing.

This is the stunted growth of Life By Default.

Default Living
Kills Creativity

◆◆◆

Are you creative?

Regardless of how you answered just now in your head, I already know the answer. You are. At least you used to be, before your ego stepped in.

Creativity means making something new. Something that didn't exist a minute ago and now it does, even if only in our mind. Creativity takes the willingness to enter into the unknown in order to bring something forth. That can feel scary, difficult, and daunting, but doesn't need to be. Just go to any preschool and you'll witness unbridled creativity. It's a beautiful thing to behold.

Not too long ago, my wife organized a painting party at our house. An artist, Stacey, came to teach us how to paint. That's at least the story I told myself. The plan was to use a famous Van Gogh painting as our inspiration. Stacey didn't give us much in the way of instruction, and I guess that was the point. She didn't even leave the copy of *Starry Night* as a reference for us to follow. She showed it to us for 20 seconds, put it away in her bag, then told us to have fun.

Within a few seconds I found myself wanting to make my painting look like the "real" *Starry Night*. I found myself Living By Default. After all, we already know what this thing is "supposed" to look like, right? Maybe not. Maybe I was missing the point.

I wasn't having fun. It wasn't until I caught a glimpse of my

4-year-old niece slapping the paint gleefully on her canvas that I realized one of us was doing it right and one of us was not. Hers looked nothing like Van Gogh's. She was doing it right.

Default living tells us how things are "supposed" to be — most likely, "the way they are now" or "the way they've always been."

Creativity tells us how things want to be.

Day by day, Life By Default kills creativity.

Default Living
Suppresses the Soul

◆◆◆

Our soulful self is our very best self, free from the trappings of the ego.

There is nothing more beautiful than a fully expressed soul. At the same time, expressing our soul is scary. We spend a lifetime hiding our soul, holding it deep inside and pushing it down, unwilling to expose it to the world. Why?

It's because the soul is the most unique aspect of ourselves and we are inherently afraid of being unique. We long to be part of something. We long to fit in. When we demonstrate our uniqueness, we feel vulnerable, and that is scary. Life By Default is much safer. Just fall in line and be sure to look like everyone else.

There's another reason why we keep our soul in check. Our soul represents a fundamental truth about who we are and our place in this world. That truth can conflict with the life that we've constructed around us. It feels as though we have to surrender important parts of our life in order to allow our souls to shine. Life By Default tells us it's too risky to pursue a life in which our soul feels free.

As a result, we get through life, but we never truly live.

Meet Your Protector

◆◆◆

Before we go any further, there's someone you need to meet. Technically, they've been with you since Day One, but you've probably never taken the time to notice. Your **Protector**. It has but one job — to keep you safe from danger. To keep you alive. Your Protector is obviously pretty good at protecting, since you're alive and well and reading this book.

But your Protector is not only concerned with keeping you safe from bodily harm. It's bent on keeping you safe from any kind of pain, disappointment or discomfort in life.

It's a big job and your Protector is good at it. In fact, your Protector has been honing its skills since the day you were born … watching your ways and studying your deepest thoughts. It knows you well, maybe even better than you know yourself. Your Protector is deeply committed to you, and only to you. Your Protector doesn't work odd jobs and isn't moonlighting on weekends. Its only job is to protect you. Sounds pretty helpful, right?

There's a problem. Your Protector sees danger at every turn. It doesn't like the unknown. Your Protector would love for you to spend every day on the couch, where it's nice and safe. Your Protector loves the default. The default is familiar. The default is safe. Whenever it gets the chance, your Protector advocates for the default.

Your Protector has been practicing these arguments for a long, long time. It knows your buttons and is not afraid to push them. Your Protector will do whatever it takes to keep you planted in your comfort zone. It's very clever.

Although very convincing, it turns out your Protector only has three basic arguments. You'll want to be on the lookout for them.

The "Not Possible" Argument

Your Protector's main objective is to convince you that whatever you are thinking about changing in your life is impossible. It will try to convince you the thing you are chasing is a unicorn. It will tell you there's no such thing as unicorns. It tells you to settle for a horse.

The "Not You" Argument

Suppose you are considering something audacious, like writing an epic novel. Or maybe you are longing to be in a deep and meaningful relationship. You can easily look around and see that other people have written epic novels, and there are lots of people in great relationships. Your Protector knows you know this so simply telling you, *it's impossible*, won't work. Instead, Your Protector tells you that it's possible, *just not for you*.

Your Protector will point out how exceptional those other people are. It will explain how lucky they must have been in order to get what they got. *You're not that lucky*, your Protector will remind you. Your Protector will remind you of all the ways you are broken and unworthy. *You're not special*, it will say. It will try to separate you from your dream of a better life, and won't stop until you stop pursuing whatever it is you're longing for.

The "Not Now" Argument

This is your Protector's last line of defense. Your Protector only uses this when the other two arguments fail. Of course, the last line of defense is the most powerful. Your Protector starts by acknowledging that your dream is possible. It then goes so far as to acknowledge that it's even possible for you, but then quickly caveats by saying ... *just not yet*. Your Protector will point out all the tools you're lacking. It will remind you of all your competing obligations. It will point out why the timing isn't right. The most insidious thing of all is it will give you a shred of hope. Your Protector will tell you the two most crushing words ever invented ... *Maybe tomorrow*.

Fortunately for us, our Protector isn't the only voice in our heads. I'll introduce you to another one in a few minutes, one you should be paying more attention to.

For now, we'll focus on your Protector. It's important for us to realize that it's not an omniscient being. Your Protector is not always right, but that's not its fault. To be fair, your Protector doesn't have to be right. It just has to avoid being wrong.

It's not your Protector's job to manage risks. Its job is to avoid them at all costs. In your Protector's mind, Life By Default is the best way to do that.

It's your job to evaluate risks.

Default Is a Choice

◆ ◆ ◆

How are you feeling about Life By Default? By now you should realize, it's no way to live. The default is convenient, sure — at least in the short-term. And it feels safe. But when you look closely, that safety is an illusion.

Because your Protector advocates for Life By Default, you might be tempted to think of it as your enemy. But it isn't. Your Protector only wants what it thinks is best for you. It suffers from a limited perspective. Your Protector is *not* the enemy.

Default is the enemy.

And Life By Default is a choice.

This is good news, actually. It means there is at least one other choice out there. In fact, you always have choices. Whether you choose to see them, let alone exercise them, is another story. When it comes to creating a better life, recognizing the opportunity for choice is **The Work**. The worst part of Life By Default isn't the resulting mediocrity that you settle for. The worst part is the feelings of powerlessness and helplessness that go along with it.

Luckily, there is an alternative.

The Default Alternative

◆◆◆

There is an alternative to choosing Life By Default. It's called, **Life By Design**.

What does "design" mean?

When we design something, we put real thought into it. We consider how the thing will be used and we allow this to inform our design decisions.

Life By Design means being intentional about the elements that you include and the elements that you exclude from your life. Life By Design means imagining the possibilities and the potential for how good things could be. Life By Design means choosing the path of maximum potential instead of the path of least resistance.

Most importantly, Life By Design means recognizing that you always have choices. They may not be obvious. They may not be easy. Nobody ever promised that life would be easy.

I can also promise that if you do The Work, if you reject Life By Default, you will feel more in control. You will feel more empowered. You will feel more satisfied. You will feel true to yourself. You will feel alive.

Choose Life By Design.

Meet the Designer

◆◆◆

Look into a mirror and introduce yourself.

When it comes to your life, there is only one person who can serve as the designer. You.

Nobody else can design our life. Too much of Life Design happens on the inside. Trusting that to someone else is a huge mistake.

Nobody else has the exact same values. Nobody else has the exact same experiences and insights that we have. Nobody has our priorities and our identical preferences. Each of us is uniquely "Me" and we can't live someone else's Life Design. It will never fit quite right.

That doesn't mean we should design our life in isolation. There are lots of stakeholders we need to take into consideration. Our family. Our friends. Our colleagues at work and the members of the various communities to which we belong. Not all perspectives are equal. Some perspectives are definitely more important than others. A good Life Design takes all of these perspectives into consideration and weighs them accordingly.

Where does God fit into this picture? Here's my take on it: God will provide the energy and courage for you to ask difficult questions and to make difficult choices. God will provide the spark of hope that keeps you going during the darkest moments. God will reveal the plan for you.

You have to do The Work yourself.

Demystifying Design

◆◆◆

What happens when you think of yourself as a designer? Does it feel intimidating? Totally unreachable? Don't worry. It did for me too.

The problem is that word, "design." We have so many examples of really good design in our lives. When we think of design, most of us think about product design, interior design, or fashion design. I'm no good at any of those. Not in a million years could I have designed the iPhone. When it comes to interior design, I'm completely useless. I have no eye for color and I never know where to put the ottoman. Sure, I know what I like when I see it, but if you left the interior design to me, it would resemble an early 1990's fraternity house.

When I look around, I'm surrounded by great designers. My wife, Kathie, has a terrific eye for design. In the house or in the garden, her choices always seem spot on. My friend Natalie makes a living using her keen eye for design by helping people create their Signature Style. Another friend, Andrea Montgomery, designs amazing jewelry. Then there's Ruth; I hired her to design the cover of this book. When it comes to their respective fields, I can't hold a candle to any of them. But when it comes to my own life, that's a different story.

There's only one great designer for that. He's got two thumbs and he's using both of them to awkwardly type this sentence.

We don't need special talent to be a competent designer of our own life. We need two things: **Intention** and **Iteration**.

Life Design Requires Intention

◆ ◆ ◆

What does it mean to be intentional? Intentional means doing something with thoughtful and purposeful action. It means acting with conscious thought and consideration. Intention means choosing, not having something chosen for you. It means not merely accepting the default.

Life By Design means consciously choosing the elements that we include and the elements that we exclude from our life. It means becoming an agent of change — someone who makes things happen, not someone to whom things happen. When we are intentional, we are the agent of change. We won't always be able to accurately predict the results, but we will be the catalyst that puts the change in motion.

To Live By Design, we must become intentional.

Life Design Requires Iteration

◆ ◆ ◆

Do you think the brilliant designs of people like Steve Jobs, Elon Musk, Donna Karan, and Frank Lloyd Wright simply popped into their heads exactly as seen in their final products? Nope. Sure, these people have great design ideas, but the final products that make their way to the public eye are never the exact original idea the designer had.

A great design idea begins as a whisper. A flash. A subtle itch that won't go away. Eventually it gets to the point where the designer can no longer stand it and resigns to do something about it. But the whispers and flashes are far from the final products we see in the world.

First designs always come up short. Always. The general public never gets to see the initial design, we only see the final design. This is why the word "design" is so intimidating for most of us. It's an artificially high bar.

The final products are the result of a design process that involves prototyping, testing, revising, re-prototyping, re-testing and revising, etc. The well-designed products that we encounter in the real world are the result of hundreds, if not thousands, of small, failed experiments. The initial creative idea is still there, but it's hidden beneath the smooth surface of the final product, as are the countless hours of failure and frustration. Real design is more about the process than the idea itself.

As you will discover, Life Design is the same.

Don't Design for Happiness

◆◆◆

So, what is the point of all this hard work? What's in it for us?

Often when I ask people what they want out of their Life Design work, the response is … *Happiness*. Seems simple enough, right? *I just want to be happy. Is that too much to ask?*

Let's dig a little deeper. For example, do we need to be happy all the time? Good luck with that. Happiness and joy are momentary emotions. The only reason we even have words for happiness and joy is because we know what it's like when we're feeling neither.

Maybe happiness is something that is measured over time? Perhaps happiness is meant to be measured over the course of an entire lifetime? Okay, fine. But that definition of happiness isn't very useful. It isn't actionable. It isn't going to help us do The Work.

Happiness is instantaneous. It's fleeting, subject to the winds and tides of the universe. If we shoot for happiness, we'll always come up short. In fact, any attempt to focus on achieving happiness mostly serves to point out the things that are making us unhappy. It's like if someone tells us not to think of a pink elephant. The pink elephant always shows up.

The pink elephant in the room is that happiness, as a life goal, is overrated. There are a few flaws with the constant pursuit of happiness. The first is that nothing is permanent. Even if we manage to get our hands on the thing that we've been longing for, someone or something will come along and break it, or change it, or take it, leaving us feeling worse than we felt before we had the thing in the first place.

Also, we are remarkably bad at predicting what will make us happy, even in the short-term. If, by chance, we do get the something that makes us happy, the happiness quickly wears off. In no time at all, we begin taking the thing for granted. I call this the **half-life of happiness**. The amount of happiness keeps getting cut in half, over and over, until it becomes negligible. That's usually about the time we discover some new thing that we imagine will make us happy, and the cycle repeats.

Don't get me wrong, there's nothing wrong with happiness. It's just not something we should strive to achieve. It's not the goal of Life Design.

If not happiness, then what?

In the next two chapters, I'll offer two alternatives to designing for happiness.

Design for Resilience

◆◆◆

Let's start with a declaration. Try this on for size…

**I can handle
absolutely any situation
that life throws my way
with poise and grace.**

Go ahead and say that to yourself a few times. Let it sink in. Say the words out loud. Use the most confident voice in your repertoire. Mine happens to be Jack Nicolson's character from *A Few Good Men*. I *can handle* the truth!

What would change if you knew this about yourself? The answer is simple. Everything.

When we believe we can handle whatever the future will bring, we can move boldly into the unknown. If life knocks us down, we know we'll bounce back up. There's a phrase in poker when you're winning big, so you're no longer worried about losing. We call it playing with "house money." **Resilience** is house money. Resilience changes everything.

It gets even better. It turns out, humans are not only incredibly resilient, we actually get stronger when our life system is disturbed. Author Nassim Nicholas Taleb calls this "anti-fragile," in his book by the same name.

Ever wonder how a vaccine works? It's not some magical elixir that prevents the bad stuff from getting into your body. The vaccine **IS** the bad stuff, just in a small dose that your body can handle. When our body detects the virus, even in small amounts, it triggers our immune system to build up a massive wall of defense that not only kills the virus but also protects us from future, larger doses. That's anti-fragile.

The concept of anti-fragility has two massive implications for our Life Design.

First, if we know that we can overcome any challenge that comes our way, it opens up a world of possibilities. We can play the game of life more aggressively because we're playing with house money.

Second, in order to get really strong, we need to design disturbances into our life system. In the introduction I mentioned my vision quest as an example of a **Designed Disturbance**, and we'll get deeper into this concept later, in Book Two - The Work.

For now, we just need to appreciate that Life Design is much more about developing resiliency than it is about trying to grasp at happiness.

Design for Authenticity

◆◆◆

Think of your favorite hero, either from fiction or from real life. What attracts you to them? Is it their accomplishments? Is it that they overcame great obstacles? Is it because they sacrificed themselves for the benefit of others? Nope.

It's because they stand for something.

They stand for themselves. Sure, your hero may be generous. Impossibly selfless, even. But when you get right down to it, every great hero has a deep connection with their true, authentic self. At the very core of their being, the hero believes in something and they have the courage to express that belief to the world.

Authenticity is attractive.

Rocky believed he was a champion. Mother Theresa believed she had to make a difference. Martin Luther King Jr. believed we're all equal.

These are real heroes, whose authenticity unfolded on a big stage in front of the entire world to witness. When authenticity unfolds on a smaller stage it is no less impressive. No less heroic.

The mother who rescues her children from an abusive spouse.

The employee who turns down a big promotion in order to pursue work they find more meaningful.

The writer who sits in front of the blank page and then

transforms it into their first novel.

The child who sings with all of her heart even though the other kids keep telling her that she has a terrible voice.

Authenticity is not a technique.

Authenticity is the center of the bullseye.

What About Purpose?

◆ ◆ ◆

People often ask me about the role of **purpose** when it comes Life Design. My answer often disappoints them, and it may well disappoint you.

Don't worry about purpose. Not Yet.

Don't get me wrong. When it comes to purpose, I'm a believer. I believe that people can discover their purpose and I often work with people to do just that. At the same time, I recognize that purpose-work is an advanced technique and most people are better off perfecting their fundamentals first.

Allow me to elaborate.

Let's start by defining what we mean by "purpose." When I talk about purpose, I'm talking about your reason for being. Why are you here? Why do you exist?

Heavy stuff, right?

Immediately these questions raise other questions. Scary questions. If I have a reason for being, where does that reason come from? How could I possibly know that? Who am I to believe that I have such a purpose? What am I supposed to do with this information anyway? What if I think I know my purpose and it turns out I have it wrong?

For those of us who are just beginning our Life Design journey, these questions are perplexing. Paralyzing. In my experience, questions like these tend to knock the fledgling Life Designer off the path rather than point the way.

I recommend we steer clear of purpose-work in the early stages. Don't worry, there will be time for discovering your true purpose. For now, I recommend we focus on **living on purpose**, which is to say, living with extreme intentionality. This approach yields more benefits in the short-term and also begins to lay an important foundation for deeper purpose-work down the road.

A few chapters from now, in Book Two - The Work, we are going to discover how to build our **inner compass**. In the early stages of Life Design, I find this to be a lot easier and a lot more useful than trying to discover one's true purpose.

The Life Design Challenge

◆ ◆ ◆

There's no question that Life Design is real work. It's a challenge. But I truly believe the payoff is well worth the effort.

So, what stands in our way?

You've met the enemy.

Our enemy has many faces.

Default thinking is the enemy.

Passive acceptance is the enemy.

Procrastination is the enemy.

Mediocrity is the enemy.

Our enemy is formidable, but not invincible.

A Different Kind of Hero

◆◆◆

With all this talk of enemies, it feels like we need a hero. Someone strong. A warrior. A fighter.

But maybe there is a better way. A better metaphor. Maybe fight and force are not what we need for this challenge. What if this isn't a battle? What if it's a journey?

For a journey, we don't need a warrior, we want an explorer. And what drives an explorer?

Curiosity.

We need the willingness to enter into the unknown, into the darkness, for the sake of discovery. The unquenchable desire to know what is knowable and to revel in the unknowable. That's curiosity.

Curiosity allows the Life Designer to ask big questions. *Why am I here?* It also allows us to ask hard questions. *What is my contribution to this particular problem? How do I need to change as a person to help the situation?* Curiosity allows us to go places we've never been before. *I wonder what will happen if...*

You might think the goal of curiosity is to create certainty. Don't fall for this devilish trick. It's true that when we allow our curiosity to guide us, learning is inevitable. Things tend to become clear when pressed by curiosity. But let's not confuse clarity with certainty. Certainty is more than elusive. It's an illusion. The goal of curiosity is not certainty.

Curiosity is the goal.

A Life Designer approaches every situation with a fierce curiosity, always asking ... *What is here for me to discover?*

The Journey Begins

◆ ◆ ◆

Congratulations! Many prospective Life Designers don't make it this far. They refuse to answer the call to adventure. I understand. Life By Default can be appealing, especially in the short-term. Life By Default means you don't have to think. You don't have to try. You don't have to care — not to the point of real action or vulnerability. You just sit back and let life happen to you. Enjoy the good times and complain about the bad. Most people live just like this.

But that's not enough for me.

Is it enough for you?

I suspect not, since you've come this far.

If you are ready, there is only one thing left to do…

Begin The Work.

BOOK TWO
—
The Work

Two Journeys

◆◆◆

Although we call it a Life Design journey, it's actually two different journeys. Yes, that's right, two.

If you look closely at any great novel or film, you will likely see the hero undertakes two different challenges. There's the external challenge that includes all of the physical, tangible, visible actions and obstacles. Rocky needed to go through a brutal training camp so that he could ultimately defeat Apollo Creed and win the heavyweight championship. Luke Skywalker worked with Yoda so that he could become a Jedi and ultimately defeat Darth Vader and the evil empire. These challenges were right there, front and center, for the world to see.

In addition to overcoming the physical challenges, Rocky and Luke had to overcome inner challenges, and these resulted in their personal transformation. In fact, it was the personal transformation that enabled both of these heroes to overcome their outer challenges. Rocky needed to believe in himself. Luke needed to learn humility and discipline. These personal transformations were as important, if not more, than the external challenges they faced.

As Life Designers, we must undertake both an **outer journey** and an **inner journey**.

Our objective, for the remainder of Book Two, is to provide you with the tools and the techniques that you will need to undertake both of these journeys.

The Inner Journey

◆◆◆

I always start with the inner journey. Unfortunately, I find that most people neglect this aspect, and instead focus on the outer journey.

I get it. The outer journey is what the rest of the world sees. The inner journey is more private and exists largely inside our own head. Focusing on the inner journey is like walking into the Corvette dealership and asking a bunch of questions about the warranty. It's a Corvette, for crying out loud! Get in. Put the top down. Smash the gas pedal.

Don't get me wrong, the outer journey is important. It includes all the things we do in the world. New jobs. New relationships. New habits. New moves. It would be silly to pretend those things are not important and exciting. But the outer journey is only half the story.

A savvy Life Designer pays equal attention to the other half too. The inner journey includes all of the ways that we must grow and develop as a person. We'll need new skills, new capacities, and new beliefs in order to make real change in our lives. It's easy to overlook this — because it feels daunting.

But it's necessary if you want to make meaningful, lasting changes.

When we're stuck in default thinking, we see everything as an external challenge. Everything is a matter of "getting" or "getting rid of" things in our life. What default thinking fails to recognize is that WE need to change.

It is the inner journey where most people stumble. The outer journey is relatively straightforward — and also involves a fair bit of luck. The inner journey requires courage and commitment. It's especially difficult to commit to a journey that you don't even know you're on.

As you imagine the life that you want to lead, ask yourself this question:

**Who will I need to become
in order to make that life possible?**

Are you ready to begin your inner journey? If you are, there's someone you need to meet.

Meet Your Guide

◆◆◆

I once heard the definition of Hell is meeting the version of yourself that you could have been, had you lived up to your full potential.

How depressing would that be? If you think your mother makes you feel guilty, how about a living reminder of every bad decision and missed opportunity, staring you right in the face? No, thank you.

But, at the same time, what if you could meet that version of yourself right now, before it's too late to change the course of your life? Imagine all that you could learn from that version of You. And no, I'm not talking about getting the next set of winning lottery numbers.

The ancient Greeks had a name for the best version of yourself. They called it Daimon. You've likely already met your Daimon. For sure you've heard its voice. It usually comes as a whisper from somewhere in the back of your mind. It's the whisper of potential and possibility.

When are you most likely to hear the quiet voice of your Daimon?

- When choosing between doing what is easy and what is right

- When deciding to forgo short-term pleasure in favor of long-term benefits

- When acting in a manner that is totally authentic, even though it may not be what the people around you want to hear

- When acting in a way that benefits someone else more than it benefits you

- When you feel pulled to make a contribution bigger than your current one. Even bigger than yourself

- When you lead by example

- When you intentionally put yourself in uncomfortable situations because you know you'll become stronger for it

- When you put yourself out there, for the world to see and to judge

- When you act from your deepest core values even though it's hard

- When you decide to break an unhealthy or unwholesome habit

- When you forgive someone, and you really mean it

- When you are the first to apologize

- When you choose to pick up the phone instead of hitting "reply"

- When you choose to Live By Design rather than Live By Default

Your Daimon's only concern is that you act from a place of your highest potential self.

Often, your Daimon will have a different opinion from your Protector. This makes sense, since they have different jobs. Ultimately, the goal is to take input from both and then decide what is best for you.

So, what is your Daimon telling you right now?

Seasons of Life

◆◆◆

Spring, summer, fall, winter. How do you prepare for the change of seasons? Of course, your answer depends on where you live. In the midwestern United States, where I live, each season practically requires an entire wardrobe swap. When I lived in Texas, we often experienced all four seasons in a single day.

When we experience the change of seasons, we plan and we adjust accordingly.

There's a similar phenomenon in Life Design. Over the next few chapters, I'm going to introduce the four basic seasons of Life Design. I sometimes refer to these as the **Four Motivations,** because they drive our behaviors and priorities.

Once we have a basic understanding of each season, we'll examine how to avoid getting caught off-guard when seasons change, and we'll learn how to actually use the seasonal changes to our benefit.

Season of Survival

◆ ◆ ◆

Have you ever found yourself at a make-or-break moment? Did it feel like everything was on the line? Did it feel like your entire existence was at stake? At its most extreme, this is the season of **Survival**.

Of course, it isn't always this extreme. The last time I experienced Survival was in the early stages of building my own business. I had left my corporate job with my annual salary, health care plan, and 401k benefits. I faced the challenge of building my brand and creating new product offerings. Most importantly, I needed to make some money so I could eat and pay my bills. To me, it was very much a survival situation.

Other people experience Survival at the loss of a job or the loss of a personal relationship. Breakups are notorious for thrusting us into Survival. Similarly, you might experience Survival with the tragic death of a close friend or family member. You might find yourself in Survival after hearing three scary words from your doctor. *You have cancer.*

There's an infinite number of scenarios that can push us into the season of Survival, but they all have one thing in common. For the person experiencing Survival, it is an all-consuming fight for your existence, metaphorically and sometimes literally. In these moments, our reality is thrown into turmoil and it's all we can do to keep from getting pulled under by the current.

In the season of Survival, there is always a notable sense of urgency. Everything feels crucial. We may suffer from tunnel vision or we may become overwhelmed by the sheer magnitude of the problems in front of us. For those who are unaccustomed to survival situations, it feels disorienting and terrifying.

Of course, great tribulations produce great heroes. The season of Survival can produce an amazing yield. In those challenging moments, we learn about ourselves. We often come to discover strengths and talents we never knew we had.

We may also discover friends and allies we never knew we had. Survival situations often bring people together to overcome a common challenge or to fight a common enemy. Survival motivation can be a powerful crucible for forming strong character and a strong community.

Some people thrive in Survival. They don't feel at home unless the heat and pressure are at record highs. In business, you often find these people in startup organizations where survival is the name of the game. Or, these survivalists gravitate toward struggling organizations or turnaround situations where their unique skills are most valued.

Although most of us don't relish being in Survival situations, it is important to note that we all have this instinct and this capability within us.

Ultimately, we are all survivors.

Season of Success

◆◆◆

We usually experience the season of **Success** when things are going well and we are inspired to make sure they keep getting better, and better, and better. For me, I experienced a season of Success that lasted nearly two decades, starting with my first job out of college.

If you could have been in my head back then, it probably would have sounded a lot like this…

The world is full of ladders and mountains, begging to be climbed. I'll plant my flag at the top for everyone to see. I thrive on accolades and adoration, as they inspire me to do even more. There's always more to do! I use words like "excellence" and "accomplishment" all the time. I set goals and I achieve them. I constantly push myself hard in order to become better, do more, and be more.

This is the season of Success.

Success is often an individual endeavor, but teamwork can be an important component as well. We can, after all, achieve more together than we can as individuals. Success often sees groups coming together to achieve remarkable results together, but in the end, it's still personal.

Success is not for everyone. Some people experience an allergic reaction to Success. They view achievement as an indulgence of the ego, as a way to separate society at a time when we should be breaking down boundaries and bringing people together. We've all met people who seem to consciously or unconsciously avoid Success.

Most people seem to enjoy the season of Success and many of us tend to get caught up in the season. Success has so much to offer, particularly in the way of material things. Success is usually pretty comfortable, unless you happen to become addicted to its many trappings.

Overall, Success is responsible for lots of great things in the world. In many ways, without Success, the next two seasons would not be possible.

Season of Significance

◆◆◆

Is this really what life is all about? What is the point of it all? Why am I here?

At one point or another, most of us have pondered questions like these. This type of inward reflection often marks the season of **Significance**.

Many people find themselves moving into Significance after a long and prosperous season of Success. Ideas of personal achievement and accomplishment start to feel less important and they become drawn toward something ... bigger.

The season of Significance is marked by a shift in priorities, from "me" to "we." The need to "accomplish" is replaced with a desire for "contribution." Someone experiencing Significance wants to contribute to the tribe, without thought or care for personal accolades and recognition.

The concept of "goals" changes during Significance. Usually in the seasons of Survival or Success our goals are super-clear and tangible. *I need to make $1000 to pay my mortgage* or *I want to get that next promotion.* In the season of Significance, our goals may be harder to pin down and measure. *I want to have a positive impact on my child's development* or *I want to leave a lasting legacy when I leave this company.*

Another way to think about it is that we measure the outcomes of Survival or Success with our eyes, but we measure the impact of Significance with our heart.

The onset of Significance looks different depending on

which aspect of our life is impacted. In our personal life, the season of Significance may see us shifting our focus from our work to our family. Professionally, this season may see us shift from focusing on our personal growth and development to becoming a mentor for others, or to becoming a great leader.

As we enter Significance, our relationship with time changes. Survival and Success are all about the here and now. We may have some concerns about the future, but with Success and Survival, it's usually not too far in the future. Matters of Significance, however, tend to take a much longer time, extending so far into the future that we often lose sight of them entirely.

Words like "impact" and "legacy" begin to take on real meaning during the season of Significance. During times of Survival or Success, these words feel hollow, irrelevant or are simply nonexistent.

For many, Significance moves at a pace that is much slower, even calming. In the early stages, Significance can be confusing and disorienting, but ultimately it can become incredibly comfortable for people who find themselves in this season.

Season of Spirituality

◆◆◆

The season of **Spirituality** is one of the rarest and least understood. This season is marked by a graceful shedding of the signs and symbols of the other seasons, like leaves falling from a tree. Things that once concerned and consumed us no longer feel important. Our concerns move beyond ourselves, beyond our tribe, beyond this lifetime, and even beyond comprehension.

When motivated by matters of Spirituality, we find ourselves concerned with matters of "transcendence." Why are we here and what happens when our time here is finished?

We begin to notice the interconnection between all things. Not only do we notice that all things are connected, we appreciate how that connection is vital.

In the season of Spirituality, the notion of "time" becomes almost meaningless. What good is a wristwatch when your concerns span infinite time? Consider the concept of "impact." Someone experiencing Success wants to have an impact and see the results right now. Someone in the season of Significance is willing to make an investment to have a positive impact on a much longer horizon. Someone in Spirituality realizes that impact is measured infinitely throughout time.

Like the other three seasons, Spirituality has unique language. Words like "purpose" and "authenticity" take on new and deeper meaning. Whereas someone in Success or Significance might have concerns about purpose and authenticity, these would likely be the means to an end. In

Spirituality, these words are fundamentally important as expressions of one's very self. Someone in the season of Spirituality is also likely to feel a deep connection to the "source" of their purpose and authenticity.

The language of Spirituality is the one that is most unlike any of the other seasons, to the point where communication becomes difficult, unless the other person has experienced Spirituality as well. For those who've never experienced a season of Spirituality, the whole thing sounds a bit confusing, maybe even silly.

No struggle to keep your head above water? No mountains to climb? No tribes? No problem.

Seasons Change

◆◆◆

When it comes to the weather, seasons are fairly predictable. Fall always follows summer. Spring follows winter. We also know roughly how long each season will last. (Though winter often overstays its welcome here in the Midwest.) For the most part, it's easy to prepare for the change that each season brings.

This isn't the case with the seasons of Life Design. They can come in any order at any time. The duration of Life Design seasons is unpredictable as well. It's not uncommon for a season to be incredibly short. I've had seasons of Survival that lasted less than a month and I experienced a season of Success that spanned two decades. Life Design seasons don't follow the *Farmer's Almanac*.

There's also no rule that says we only experience one Life Design season at a time. In fact, most people discover they are living two or three seasons simultaneously. It's entirely possible to be living all four at the same time, which can make for some challenges when it comes to dressing appropriately! There's also no guarantee that we will experience every season. Some people go a lifetime and never experience all four seasons. Everyone's experience of the Life Design seasons is unique.

That said, there are some things we can watch for that will help us to notice and negotiate the seasons of Life Design.

Rolling with the Changes

◆◆◆

It's great that we've identified these different seasons, but what now? How do we use this information to help us with our Life Design goals?

Well, if I told you I'm taking you on a surprise trip this weekend and you should go pack your bags, what is the first thing you'd ask me? You'd want to know where we are going, of course. Otherwise, you'd have no idea how to pack. The same logic applies here.

Take a look at your Life Design goals. Which season feels most appropriate for where you want to go? You may have been living comfortably in one season but the place you want to go is likely to bring a totally different experience. For example, for most of my adult life I told myself that I had no interest in being in a long-term relationship. Relationships complicate things and I was focused on climbing the ladders of Success. Relationships are much more about Significance, so I needed to learn some new things.

When we experience a new Life Design season, it's not as simple as throwing on a pair of shorts or adding a sweater. The new season can feel completely foreign to us. It's as if we have to learn how to BE in the new season. It takes time. It takes practice. It takes patience.

A good Life Designer understands the seasons from every angle. A Life Designer knows which seasons are the most comfortable and which ones may bring challenges. A Life Designer recognizes when a new season is approaching. A Life Designer listens closely, because sometimes the seasons call to us, like a whispered invitation. Sometimes we have to move towards the season rather than waiting for the season to come to us.

Additional Resources

To help you better understand and recognize how the four seasons show up in your life, we've created a series of **Seasonal Energy Assessments**.

You can access the Digital Appendix here:
www.nevertoolatebook.com

Building Your Compass

◆ ◆ ◆

Have you ever found yourself in a heavy fog or a white-out snowstorm? I'm talking zero visibility. It's impossible to move when you can't see your path. Have you ever experienced the disorienting phenomenon of being in a vast desert where everything around you looks the same? It also happens when you're deep in the woods and totally surrounded by tall trees or heavy brush. You completely lose your sense of direction.

In the early stages of Life Design, people often struggle because they don't know where they want to go. They just know they want to go somewhere. Our brain doesn't appreciate the contradiction, so we shut down. We slip into default thinking and simply stay put. It's easier to stick with what we know.

How do we overcome the unsettling feeling of wanting to be somewhere else without knowing exactly where we want to be?

That's where our compass comes in.

In this age of GPS-enabled smart phones, most of us have never tried to navigate by compass. It feels like it should be easy. The compass always points north. What could be simpler?

It turns out, simple isn't always easy.

I remember my first lesson in compass navigation. It came during a weeklong wilderness survival training course. My instructor took me to a high peak and pointed to another peak about 2 miles away.

"I'll meet you there," he said as he walked off into the trees.

I excitedly whipped out my compass and quickly discovered that my destination was due east of where I was standing. This was going to be easy. I put the compass in my pocket because I wouldn't even need it. Famous last words.

Thirty minutes later I found myself deep in the valley, surrounded by dense trees. I could no longer see the peak that was my destination. Moving was difficult. Heavy brush and uneven terrain prevented me from walking in a straight line. I spent most of my time walking in every direction but east. West to get across that stream. North to avoid the poison ivy. South because I saw something that I thought might be a bear. After every diversion I had to reorient myself to my easterly heading. Eventually, I made it. Of course, my instructor was already there, swinging lazily in his hammock and laughing at my misfortune.

As difficult as it was, I could never have made it without my compass.

The beauty of a compass is that it tells us which direction we are headed, even if we can't see our destination. Compass navigation allows us to move around obstacles without losing our overall sense of direction. Our compass tells us which way we're pointing, even when we are deep in the thick of things.

You need a compass. There will be times in your Life Design journey when you have a specific destination in mind. *I'm going to get to that rock on the top of that hill.* Your compass will help you choose your destinations wisely. Your compass will also help keep you on track as you deal with inevitable diversions. *Oh wait, there's a bear between me and that rock and I think I'll keep my distance.*

You won't use your compass every day, but you'll have it with you every day. Having it in your pocket will be source of comfort and confidence. Knowing how to use it will be even more so.

Let's build you a compass.

What's Your Mojo?

◆◆◆

In the wilderness, every compass points north. When it comes to Life Design, our compasses don't all point in the same direction. We each need to figure out what our figurative "north" should be. How do we figure out what our Life Design compass should point toward?

One way is to orient towards our **mojo**. Our mojo is our passion. The thing we would do if we were completely free of obligations and obstacles. The things that make our heart sing.

Don't know what — or where — that is yet? Don't worry. There are a few ways to find it.

My brother, Carl, spent the first 28 years of his professional career as an electrical engineer. In his late 40s, he found that he no longer had the drive and passion that he once had for the work. What used to feel like a challenge now felt challenging. Carl needed a change and he knew it.

He went into a deep stage of self-reflection and, in doing so, Carl began to realize that most of his mojo moments took place outdoors. Fishing. Camping. Mountain biking. If he wasn't outdoors, Carl often spent his leisure time reading about the outdoors or watching documentary films about nature. When he watched the news or read the papers, he found his mind drawn to stories about the environment.

Nature was Carl's mojo. Twenty years later, Carl has redesigned his life so that his mojo is front and center. No longer an electrical engineer, he now works in the filed of environmental conservation and he can barely remember the years spent slogging through project plans and counting the minutes until the end of his workday. He comes home now feeling exhausted, but fulfilled. Know why? Because Carl is using his compass to point him in *his right direction*: toward his mojo.

To find your mojo, think about some of the peak experiences you've had in your personal or professional life. There are a few ways to recognize **mojo moments** in your life. These are times when:

- You felt completely alive, full of energy and enthusiasm.

- You were able to DO without having to TRY.

- You accomplished something you didn't think you could.

- You worked with others as a team in a seamless, natural way.

- You were so immersed in an activity that you lost track of time.

- You were willing to put in extremely hard work to prepare for something because you knew it mattered.

- You acted from a place of selfless generosity.

The cool thing about mojo moments is they sear into our memory. We can transport ourselves right back into our mojo moments, almost reliving the experience in real time. That's exactly what we want to do, so we can understand our mojo moments and ultimately incorporate the essence of these experiences into our Life Design. So, ask yourself...

What allowed these mojo moments to happen? What were the circumstances? What was your role? Who else was involved? Has it ever happened again? As you think through your Life Design goals, look to these Mojo Moments for inspiration, motivation, and direction. Add them to your compass.

Because mojo matters.

Additional Resources

Check out the **What's Your Mojo?** worksheet, available in the Digital Appendix.

You can access the Digital Appendix here: www.nevertoolatebook.com

Who's Your Hero?

◆◆◆

So far, we've been building your compass by looking inward. It's also helpful to look outside of ourselves, to examine the stories that are all around us.

Stories are powerful. We know this because there are stories that have endured for millennia. A good story connects with us on a deep level. It's said that we see in stories what we want to see in our own lives.

The Fountainhead, by Ayn Rand, is my favorite book of all time, mostly because I am so drawn to the main character, Howard Roarke. He's an architect who struggles in the world because he chooses to follow his heart rather than the conventions of the time. Throughout the book, Roarke is criticized and even ostracized because of his deep and unwavering commitment to his ideals. I like to think, on my very best days, I've got a bit of Howard Roarke in me.

We see in stories what we want to see in our own lives.

What are your favorite stories? Who are your heroes, real and imagined, and what can they tell you about the story you want to write for yourself?

Add them to your compass. Let them help point the way.

◆◆◆

Additional Resources

Check out the **Who's Your Hero?** worksheet, available in the Digital Appendix at www.nevertoolatebook.com

Your Superpower

◆◆◆

What is your **superpower**?

When I ask this question to business executives, I'm often met with blank stares. People don't think of themselves as having a superpower. At least not in the sense of Superman or Wonder Woman.

What if we change the language a bit? What if, instead of your superpower, I ask you to identify your talent and abilities that allow you to make a unique contribution? What makes you special in your role within whatever organization you care about?

I find that many people resist the very idea of being "special." It feels narcissistic. It feels unhealthy. We notice all the people around us with inflated egos and we know that's not how we want to be seen in the world. It doesn't need to be this way. We can have a deep understanding and appreciation for our uniqueness and still be a good person. In fact, it's crucial that we do this. In order to be part of something, we must completely understand our part.

No matter what we are doing in the world, there is always someone else who could do the same thing, maybe, in some ways, better than we do it. But nobody will do it exactly the same way that we do it. Understanding this uniqueness allows us to focus our efforts. It allows us to seek out opportunities where our uniqueness makes all the difference. Once we appreciate our uniqueness, others will begin to appreciate it too.

This is where the benefits of our superpower really kick in.

How often do you get to use your superpower to help others? Do you get to use it every day? Or, is it something that you only get to use on a rare occasion, like when someone is robbing a bank under a blue moon?

Is there a way that you can design your life so that you get to use your superpower every single day?

◆ ◆ ◆

Additional Resources

Check out the **Discovering Your Superpower** worksheet, in the Digital Appendix.

You can access the Digital Appendix here: www.nevertoolatebook.com

Your Personality Topography

◆◆◆

A topographical map is one of the most useful types, because it shows elevation changes, and this is very helpful when planning your route. If there are two routes that both get me to my desired destination and one of them requires a 3,000-foot climb with a treacherous descent whereas the other one is a slow gentle downslope the whole way, I know which one I'm going to take.

When it comes to Life Design, the terrain that we're most interested is ourselves. Our **personality topography**. Our brain. Our tendencies. Our preferences. Our biases. The goal is to understand what kinds of challenges our interior terrain is going to cause us along the way.

Are you a perfectionist who's going to struggle with the whole concept of frequent experiments and embracing failure? Are you a high-energy adventurer who loves to move quickly from one experience to the next, but may have trouble focusing on any one thing for very long?

None of this is bad, mind you. It's who you are. I have my own qualities and quirks too. We all do. It's a matter of understanding our personality topography so that we can adjust our approach accordingly.

There are a lot of maps out there that will give you a sense of your personality topography. These maps can help you understand how you see and make sense of the world. Which map will work for you is largely personal preference.

I always say that some map is better than no map.

That said, two of my favorite maps for Life Design purposes are the Enneagram and Clifton Strengths Finder.

Both of these maps can help you to better understand your motivations and your talents, which is incredibly useful as you begin to plan your Life Design journey.

A Life Designer practices with many different maps and chooses the right one for the occasion.

Additional Resources

We've provided a list of different topographical maps in the Digital Appendix.
Check out the **Personality Topography** worksheet, available in the Digital Appendix.

You can access the Digital Appendix here:
www.nevertoolatebook.com

Sharpening Your Axe

◆◆◆

" Give me six hours to cut down a tree,
I'll spend the first four sharpening the axe.

\- Abraham Lincoln

This is often what the inner journey feels like to fledgling Life Designers. We've lived with our default lives for so long and we're ready for change. I get it. I've been there. I also know what it's like when you get out into the wilderness and realize you've forgotten your water purifier. Shit happens. But I'm going to try to keep you out of it.

Spending some time on the inner journey, learning about the changing seasons, building your personal compass, and studying your personality topography, is the best way I know how to prepare you for what's to come.

The outer journey.

The Outer Journey

◆◆◆

We've arrived at everyone's favorite part of the program
... *just tell me how to do it!*

If you've been paying attention, you know it's not going to
be that simple. The good news is that most people find the
outer journey to be the most exciting part. Probably because
it's here that most people start to feel like they are making
real progress toward their Life Design goals. The results of
the outer journey are more tangible and more visible to us,
but also to the rest of the world. Not that we care what other
people think, right?

So, let's get into it. The outer journey is really about
answering four crucial questions:

Where am I right now?

This might feel obvious, but most people don't have a really
solid orientation when it comes to understanding what is
working, what isn't, and why. If we want to go somewhere,
we have to know where we are starting from.

Where do I want to go?

Some people have absolutely no idea where they want to get
to with their Life Design. They know "here" isn't working
for them, but they don't know where "there" is. Other
people have an incredibly precise idea of where they want
to go, and this precision actually gets in their way.

What's Stopping Me?

Encountering obstacles is inevitable on our Life Design journey. Some of the obstacles we encounter will be real and others will be figments of our overactive imagination. We'll learn how to tell the difference and how to handle obstacles of every shape and size.

How do I get there?

Getting into motion is one thing. Making sure we are moving in the right direction and stay moving in the right direction is quite another. We'll talk about all of it.

These are the questions the outer journey is meant to answer. Are you ready to figure out your answers?

Where Am I Now?

◆ ◆ ◆

A wise old fish swims past two younger fish and says, "How's the water, boys?" A few seconds later, the two young fish turn toward each other and one of them says, "What's water?"

Before we can begin our outer journey, we need to get outside of the fishbowl and notice the water we've been swimming in all these years.

A Quick Assessment

◆◆◆

On a scale from 1 to 10, how would you rate your life overall?

Do you find it difficult to assign a single rating? Our lives are so complex, how can we possibly boil it down to a single number and have that be meaningful? On top of that, it's hard to choose a rating with no frame of reference. What makes for a 1? What makes for a 10? Even if we come up with a score, what are we going to do with that? It doesn't tell us very much. It's not a very good question. Try this one...

On a scale from 1 to 10, how would you rate the state of your physical health?

It feels different, right? A bit more solid. By narrowing the focus to just one aspect of our lives, we create a sort of picture-puzzle of our existence. Our brain immediately wants to fill in the missing pieces.

What are the other pieces, and how are *they* going? Most likely you have some immediate thoughts.

I am so out of shape; I feel like absolute crap.

My health is fine, it's my marriage that's in shambles.

My job is okay, it pays well, but it doesn't do anything for my soul. And so on.

As soon as we begin thinking about this, we immediately try to self-diagnose. We immediately begin trying to solve the problems. It's almost impossible to stop ourselves. It's our nature to figure things out.

As we start to fill in all the pieces of the puzzle, something unexpected happens. We start to develop a frame of reference that helps us better understand each part. We get a sense of how each area is doing relative to the other areas, thus giving us a better understanding of our life as a whole.

What do you say we do a complete inventory of your whole life, right now?

Don't worry, we'll keep this really simple. No fancy tests or complicated questions; all you need is a piece of paper and something to write with. (If you prefer, you can use the worksheets available in the Digital Appendix*.)

Write the following categories along one side:

Health

Work

Finances

Relationships

Personal Growth

Fun!!!

Spirituality

Then, for each of the seven areas of your life, simply assign a rating: Green (Feeling great), Yellow (Could be better), Red (Needs Attention) rating.

There you have it. That's the current state of your Life Design. The good, the bad, and the somewhere-in-between. That didn't hurt too much, did it? What did you discover?

* Additional Resources

Check out the **A Quick Assessment** worksheet, available in the Digital Appendix.
To go deeper in any one of the areas, check out the **Deep Dive Assessments,**

You can access the Digital Appendix here:
www.nevertoolatebook.com

A Good Hammer

◆ ◆ ◆

Is there at least one area of your life that you rated Green? It can be hard to see the bright side when things are not going very well. But even in the darkest times, we can find one or two bright spots. Start there.

Most people want to jump right to their problem areas. I get it. Those are the areas that hurt. Before we go there, we want to examine the areas of your life that are going better.

Please allow me to explain … If I asked you to pick up a suitcase off the floor, which hand would you use? Chances are, you'd start with your dominant hand. You don't know if the case is empty or filled with gold bullion. We default to using our strengths whenever we can. We're wired to win.

The areas you rated as Green are likely your areas of greatest strength, talent, and capacity. When problems arise, these are probably the places you go first, because we lead with our strengths. We default to our comfort zones.

The corollary to this rule is that we tend to neglect the areas where we are weak. Unfortunately, this means we never get stronger in these areas. Instead, we compensate for our weaknesses by leaning more on our strengths.

This makes us even stronger in the areas where we were already strong, adding to the overall imbalance.

There's an old saying: *When your best tool is a hammer, everything looks like a nail.*

Life Designers recognize not everything is a nail.

Embrace the Pain

◆ ◆ ◆

Just as we each have areas of our lives that are going well, somewhere in our life, there is pain. People don't buy books like this one when everything is coming up roses.

So, tell me where it hurts.

Are you feeling a twinge of apprehension?

Society tells us that we're not supposed to tell people we're in pain. Pain is a sign of vulnerability. Pain is a sign of weakness, right?

No. Pain is an indicator that something isn't right with the world. Period.

Avoiding pain is the true sign of weakness.

Our default reaction is to move away from pain. We flinch even when we think there's going to be pain. We get as far away as we can so whatever it is can't hurt us. If we get far enough from the source of pain, we can ignore it.

Life Designers don't flinch. Life Designers move toward the pain. Life Designers seek to better understand it and to work with the pain. Life Designers know that pain is crucial to understanding.

What's your pain? Is it stress? Is it a feeling of being lost or stuck? Is it a deep longing for something different in your life? Whatever it is, that is your personal pain. Don't bother comparing your pain to other people's, because it doesn't matter. What matters is your pain and how it feels to you.

Pain is good. Pain shows us the areas of our lives that need attention. Pain creates the motivation for change. Don't ignore the pain or simply compensate for it by defaulting to your strengths.

Move toward the pain. Embrace it.

Embrace the pain.

Draw Connections

◆◆◆

Life is complex. Paradoxically, the more you understand about the world, the more complex it becomes. Ask your average 4-year-old about the complexities of life and you're likely to get some profound wisdom dropped on you. We're talking Zen Koan-level stuff. Four-year-olds don't see complexity.

The same holds true for many people at the end of life. In the final months of my father's battle with Alzheimer's, he spent his time walking the halls with an imaginary flashlight looking for maintenance issues he could fix. Life was incredibly complex for everyone around him, but for him, things were pretty simple.

This isn't simply a case where ignorance is bliss, though. Life really is complex, whether we're oblivious to that fact or not. A fair amount of our daily problems are the result of our failure to notice this complexity. We fail to see how the different areas of our lives interact and impact one another.

Some of us focus too much of our energy and attention on work, so our personal relationships suffer. The fact that we're only working so hard so that we can provide for our family doesn't stop those relationships from suffering the most.

Some of us stress out about our finances to the point where it makes us physically ill, which makes us less capable of doing the things we need to do to improve our financial situation. Or we can't afford to do fun things to relieve stress, which causes the stress to build and build.

Some of us work our entire lives, dreaming of the freedom that will come with retirement, only to discover that our work was a primary source of purpose and direction in our lives. Without it, we find ourselves feeling useless and without direction.

When it comes to our life system, the connections are often subtle. Rarely is there a direct and obvious cause-effect relationship. Unfortunately, most of us don't do subtle very well. We much prefer the obvious. We like clear cause and effect. When I do X, I get Y result. To understand the subtle connections, we need to put our lives under a magnifying glass.

Take some time to notice the connections. Notice the things that are going well, and how those things are related. Notice the things that are not going well, and how they are related. Notice how the good and the not so good are also intertwined. We like to think of the different parts of our lives as neatly separated, when in fact, they are fundamentally connected.

Life Designers are skilled at drawing connections.

Additional Resources

Check out the **Draw Connections** worksheet, available in the Digital Appendix.

You can access the Digital Appendix here:
www.nevertoolatebook.com

The Myth of "Balance"

◆◆◆

I want to spend a hot minute on the notion of work-life balance. Everyone wants work-life balance. If I ask 10 corporate executives what they want, 9 of them say work-life balance.

Screw work-life balance. If the last chapter teaches us anything it's that seeking *balance* is the wrong way to go about this.

Balance implies counteractive forces that must be kept in a state of equilibrium. In a system as interconnected and interdependent as our life-system is, balance is a myth.

Harmony is the goal. One voice complements the other. It's not a competition. It's not a trade-off. It's a complete system that must be examined and understood as such.

Life Designers are excellent harmonizers.

Shift Happens

◆◆◆

Truly diagnosing the pain requires us to go back to the point where the pain began. Can you remember a time when things were going well? What was different then? What has changed about the environment since? How have you changed? What about the people around you? How have they changed? Most likely, you'll notices changes in multiple areas. If there's one constant in the universe, it's that things constantly change.

Why is change a problem? Inherently, change isn't bad. So why does change get such a bad rap?

There are three scenarios where change kicks our butt. (1) When we fear change so much that we remain in the default, even though it sucks. (2) When we fail to notice the change happening and we end up blindsided. (3) When we see the change happening, but we fight the change rather than invest the time and energy to embrace it.

How have you dealt with the changes in your life? Did you fall into any of the traps I just mentioned? Maybe more than one of them? Don't beat yourself up. We all do it.

Don't blame yourself. In fact, don't blame anyone. It's important to resist the urge to lay blame. Blame is the default way of making sense of a confusing situation. We blame others. We blame the universe. We blame God. Some of us even blame ourselves. Don't bother. Blame is a waste of time and a waste of energy. Blame is about judgment, and Life Design is about making progress.

As you look back over the changes that have unfolded, remind yourself that you made the best decisions that were available to you at the time that you made them. And everyone else did too.

Our reason for looking to the past is to identify useful information for designing a better future.

Life Designers know that shift happens, and they are more than willing to get into it.

Additional Resources

Check out the **Shift Happens** worksheet, available in the Digital Appendix.

You can access the Digital Appendix here: www.nevertoolatebook.com

Where Am I Going?

◆ ◆ ◆

If Henry Ford had asked his contemporaries what they wanted to improve transportation, they would have said, "Faster horses."

"Faster horses" is default thinking.

What do you want from your Life Design? Why do you want it? These seem like simple questions, but they are deceptively difficult. We are really good at noticing when things are broken or causing us pain, but we're not very good when it comes to envisioning a better future. For most of us, our brains think incrementally. *It hurts and I want it to stop hurting.*

Surely, we can do better than that. Right?

As we've discussed, Life Design is about developing **resiliency** and achieving **authenticity**. The problem is, that's a lot like declaring, "I'm hungry" and "I'm thirsty." Great. Would you like an açai bowl and some sparkling water or are you leaning toward a pizza and some beer? Unfortunately, I know my own answer. The possibilities are endless and too much choice tends to paralyze us.

It's also tough to envision a better future when your present situation stinks. The problems of today always take priority. You spend all of your energy simply trying to keep your head above water. Focusing only on today's problems is default thinking.

So … What do you want from your Life Design and why?

Another reason these two questions are difficult to answer is that we become numb to life. We desensitize when it comes to the little annoyances in our lives. We learn to live with them. We make the best of a bad situation. That's a good thing, right? Sort of. Making the best of a bad situation is an excellent short-term strategy, but we lose sight of the big picture.

Figuring out where we want to go with our Life Design is not easy. But we can't get to a better place without having some sense of where we want to go. The next three chapters will offer some techniques for figuring that out.

More Or Less

◆ ◆ ◆

What did your 7-year-old self want to be when you grew up? Back then it was easy. *A doctor. An astronaut. A teacher. President.*

Somewhere along the way, it got complicated. It was no longer about the basic, instinctual desires. It wasn't about curiosity and it definitely wasn't about fun. Somewhere along the way we introduced all kinds of rules and requirements, and these constrained our imagination.

Years later, we can't make any decisions without thinking about "the rules." We can't move without considering all of the implications. We can't think outside the box. We default to the box. The box is comforting.

We need to design our way out of the box.

But opening up our imaginations to the infinite realm of possibilities is not easy. In fact, imposing that kind of pressure on ourselves when thinking about our desired future can make the whole system shut down. We become paralyzed by possibility. *What if there is something out there I can't even imagine? What if I make a mistake?*

There is. And you will.

Ask a child what they want in their life and you'll get an immediate, definitive answer. But we're adults. We need to respect our adult (adulterated?) minds and take things at a responsible, adult-like pace. Slowly.

I'm going to make this really simple. Kindergarten-math simple. Try these two questions on for size:

What do you want more of in your life?

What do you want less of in your life?

Notice how the phrasing of the question forces us away from specific solutions. We don't want to become the next assistant to the regional manager, we want more recognition and autonomy at work. Thinking in terms of *more* or *less* brings a useful level of abstraction to the conversation.

Life Designers know that sometimes less is more.

Additional Resources

Check out the **More Or Less** worksheet, available in the Digital Appendix.

You can access the Digital Appendix here:
www.nevertoolatebook.com

But Why?

◆ ◆ ◆

If you've spent any amount of time with a 4-year old, you know their favorite word is "why?" They are supremely curious, and they know you have the answers. Of course, no matter what answer you give, the response is always the same. "Why?" It's a never-ending loop.

As annoying as this may be when you're focused on driving, or, trying to get the 4-year old to clean up their room, there's really something beautiful happening here. With each subsequent "why?" you get closer and closer to the *real* reason. This is what I call "bedrock." Here's an example…

I want to lose 20 pounds.

Why?

I want to be healthier.

Why?

I want to be able to live longer.

Why?

I want to be there for my family as long as I can.

Or…

I want to find a new job.

Why?

I want a new boss.

Why?

My boss treats me like crap.

Why is that important to you?

I want to be treated with dignity and respect.

Or...

I want a new job.

Why?

They don't value my contribution.

Why is that important to you?

I want to feel like I'm having an impact.

Why?

Because if you have to work, you might as well derive some kind of personal meaning from it.

Usually, four "Whys?" is enough to reach bedrock.

Go ahead, try it. Start with the first thing you want more of in your life, and drill down into the "Whys?" until you hit bedrock.

Now take a look at your initial desire and compare it to your bedrock answer. Can you feel how much more basic, how much more essential your bedrock response is than your original response?

Once we've identified our **essential desire**, we might find there are other ways to achieve it. Whereas our initial response may have focused exclusively on a specific solution or course of action, our essential desire is more thematic, which means we have more flexibility on how to go about it. We might also notice that our essential desire shows up in other areas of our life as well, which is a bonus.

Here's a tip … We can use the ideas we came up with during the "More or Less" exercise with the "Four Whys" technique. You might find that you come up with more potent language to describe your ideas. Instead of "more money" you might find that you really want "financial stability." Or instead of "more sex" you might want "more connection." Can you feel how this shift in language might actually change your approach to going after these things?

Life Designers always ask "Why?"

Additional Resources

Check out the **But Why?** worksheet, available in the Digital Appendix.

You can access the Digital Appendix here:
www.nevertoolatebook.com

Identify Themes,
Not Goals

◆ ◆ ◆

What's the longest you've ever maintained a New Year's Resolution? I suspect most resolutions don't see the light of February. What's up with that? Is it a lack of willpower? Do we only *think* we want change, but when it comes right down to it, we really just want to stay exactly where we are?

Nah. I give us more credit than that. I blame bad design.

I used to set resolutions for myself that were unachievable. Sometimes the goals were just too ambitious and as soon as I realized this, I abandoned the goal entirely.

I'm going to write and publish two novels this year.

Sometimes my resolution required me to maintain a streak and once I broke the streak, there was no point in continuing.

I'm going to read one book each week.

Sometimes I set a goal that was really specific only to realize that I didn't really want what I thought I wanted. Or my priorities changed.

I'm going to get six-pack abs.

Then, I changed the way I approach my New Year's Resolution process. Instead of a specific goal, I began identifying a single word that would encapsulate my aspirations for the new year. The word, in a sense, became a theme for the year. From there, I need only check in with myself every couple of weeks to see how I'm doing with regards to my theme. I write my word on a Post-it note and stick it on my bathroom mirror. I make it my screensaver. I share my word with the most important people in my life and I ask them to be on the lookout for evidence, or lack thereof, that I'm living my word.

The year that I met my wife, my word was "Bold." The year that I left the corporate world in order to pursue my own professional path, my word was "Authenticity." The year that I started to make real progress with my business-building was the year that I chose "Connection."

What's your word? What's your aspiration?

Life Designers appreciate the power of a kick-ass theme.

What's Stopping Me?

♦♦♦

There's an old parable about training circus elephants that is often used in the context of personal growth and development. It goes like this...

If you chain a baby elephant to a stake, the he will quickly learn that he can go only so far before the chain stops his progress. He'll tug at the chain a few times, but eventually he'll come to realize the boundaries of his captivity. Years later, when the elephant is fully grown to the point where no chain could stop him if he wanted to move, he still won't test his chains. He has been conditioned to accept the limitations that he once knew to be real.

Have you tested your chains lately?

The Myth of "Too Busy"

◆◆◆

Once we start to get serious about changing our life, we will suddenly realize how busy we are. This is the same whether we are the type of person who is perpetually busy or if we are just hyper-vigilant about managing our workload. The feeling of being too busy is our Protector's last-ditch effort to convince us that it's not the right time to make a change. It will whisper in our ear … *Not now.*

Don't listen to your Protector about this. You are the only one who gets to decide if it is the right time or not. Here's the secret: It's the right time to do *something*. The fact that you are even asking the question proves it. That doesn't mean you need to do everything, but it's always the right time to do something.

Life Designers are busy. We all are. But Life Designers are never too busy.

Time for a Detox

◆ ◆ ◆

Life Design is often about adding new things to our life, but sometimes the biggest gains can be found in simple elimination. Eliminating something often takes a lot less time and we may find that we actually have more available resources afterward. Eliminating the right thing can be life changing.

I use the analogy of **toxins** for this because the things that need to be eliminated are usually pretty subtle, and their negative effects accumulate slowly over time. Likewise, toxins can be so subtle as to avoid detection. That is, unless we are specifically looking for them.

Toxins in our Life Design are anything that is unnecessarily draining our resources. By resources, I'm talking about anything from our finances to our time, attention, and energy. Here are some common toxins:

- Unhealthy or unsupportive relationships

- Unhealthy habits

- Unnecessary, recurring expenses

- Social commitments that no longer serve your goals or interests

- Annoying but necessary tasks that you've been procrastinating

- Large projects that you can't seem to finish

For our purposes, toxins are things that we can eliminate from our life with relative ease. We're looking for quick-hit solutions here. For example, you probably wouldn't want to identify "your job" as a toxin, because presumably eliminating your job tomorrow is not an option. You might, however, identify one aspect of your job that is toxic and do something about that. Perhaps there is a particular person with whom you work on a regular basis that you find to be toxic. You might work to reduce your exposure to that person.

The goal is to eliminate the toxins we can cut out relatively easily and without much effort, so we can quickly free up the energy and resources that we're going to need to do the real work of Life Design.

Additional Resources

For a list of common toxins, check out the **Detox List**, available in the Digital Appendix.

You can access the Digital Appendix here:
www.nevertoolatebook.com

Immovable Objects

◆◆◆

Watasi wa nihongo ga hanase masen.

I can't speak Japanese.

Because I can't, it is incredibly unlikely that I'm going to get my dream job as the U.S. ambassador to Japan.

Sometimes the problems or challenges that we face in our life will be like this. I call them **immovable objects**. Don't spend a lot of energy pushing on immovable objects.

That is, if they are indeed immovable.

Sometimes we mistakenly think an object is immovable, so we never bother to push. This is what it means to Live By Default. We assume the fundamental nature of the obstacle in front of us, but we never test that assumption.

From time to time, we encounter an obstacle that is standing between the life we have right now and the life we would like to have, and we've convinced ourself that it's immovable. So we never push on it. We simply throw our hands up in the air and declare defeat.

But what if pushing isn't the only option?

Reframe the Problem

◆◆◆

To understand this next concept, I'd like to introduce you to John. When John was about 24 years old, he was diagnosed with epilepsy. At the time, he was a long-haul truck driver. He loved everything about that job and he was devastated when doctors told him the anti-seizure medication would mean giving up his commercial driver's license. John had a problem. A big problem.

I can't drive my truck anymore because of my medical condition.

Fact. Immovable object. Can you feel it? The way this problem statement is framed, it's unsolvable. Imagine if you were John, looking at the world through that lens. Pretty depressing, right? What if John was able to reframe the problem differently?

Since I can't drive my truck anymore, I need to find a job that doesn't require me to drive.

What do you feel now? More room to move, right? It's so simple that it feels obvious. I assure you it isn't. Not when the problem is yours. When it's your problem your brain automatically defaults to an unfavorable frame. Why? Because it's convenient. It removes all responsibility to solve the problem. It's so much easier to simply scream, at the top of our lungs, "Life sucks!"

Indeed. Life sucks, sometimes. Then we move on.

I can't get the job as the U.S. ambassador to Japan. That sucks.

I need to learn Japanese well enough that I can get an entry-level position at the U.S. consulate in Japan. *That's* a challenge.

What problem are you trying to solve? Have you framed it in such a way that it is impossible to solve? It's time to design a problem statement that can be solved.

Differentiate Fact
From Belief

◆◆◆

This feels so simple and obvious. Yet, we routinely mistake our beliefs for fact. When most people say "fact," what they really mean is "deeply held, personal belief."

Here's one way to differentiate. Facts are the same for everyone, from every angle. When it comes to real life, facts are rare and facts are boring. Chicago is north of Indianapolis. Okay. So what? There's really nothing to discuss, right?

It's only when facts are called into question that something interesting happens. If you ever want to experience the frustration that comes from the fine line between fact and belief, go to YouTube and search for "Flat Earth."

When everyone agrees, facts become the default position. That's a good thing. We don't waste precious time and energy rediscovering things that are generally accepted.

When our beliefs go un-examined, they also become the default position. That's where we get into trouble. Because beliefs are not facts. We may miss an opportunity because our beliefs tell us that something is impossible.

Beliefs are the truth as we see it, from our perspective. Our truth. Nothing more. We may hold these beliefs to be very deep and dear to us, but they are still beliefs. But beliefs sure do feel a lot like facts. In the end, what's the difference?

The difference is in what we do with the information. The adult elephant believes the chain is strong enough to hold him back. The belief becomes his truth.

Beliefs are operative. They affect our behavior. Beliefs can be limiting or enabling, depending on whether they constrain or inspire us to take action.

Enabling beliefs, such as the belief that we can overcome a challenge, are almost always beneficial. Demonstrating our belief in someone else can have a similar, enabling effect for the other person. Generally speaking, enabling beliefs do good work in the world. In my experience, the only time that enabling beliefs get people into trouble is when they are completely unchecked and completely unsubstantiated. I truly believed that I could ride that mechanical bull on the "El Diablo" setting. That was an unsubstantiated belief.

Limiting beliefs almost always cause damage. We believe in our mind and in our heart that we can't do something, so we don't. Limiting beliefs keep us Living By Default.

Limiting beliefs disguise themselves as facts and invite themselves into our living room. Actually, it's more like our basement, because most of the time we don't even know that limiting beliefs are present.

Because it is so difficult to recognize our own limiting beliefs, we usually need an outside perspective. Share your story with someone you trust. Ask that person if they can identify any beliefs that you have about yourself that might be holding you back, particularly if they don't believe the same thing.

A word of warning here. Keep in mind the person you ask might share the same limiting beliefs as you.

When trying to identify your limiting beliefs, you really need multiple perspectives. I'll offer this general guideline to keep in mind…

If you find *two or more* who holds a different belief than you, it's worth considering there might be more to the story. This is not to say that your belief is wrong, but that you should look very closely to make sure your Protector isn't advocating for a limiting belief on your behalf.

The next few chapters will show you some other techniques for working with your limiting beliefs.

I Can't vs. I Won't

◆◆◆

Think of something that you'd like to change, and then think of something that is stopping you from making that change. Got it?

Where is the thing that's stopping you located?

Chances are, you identified something that is "out there." Outside of you. Beyond your control. Our default mind prefers obstacles that are outside of us because externalities are convenient scapegoats. We can blame the economy, we can blame our bosses, we can blame the weather, and so on. As long as it isn't something wrong with us, then we're off the hook. We can remain as we are right now, guilt-free.

The problem is that it's hardly ever about the externalities. It almost always comes down to us and how badly we want the change. The obstacles between our ears are always more formidable than the obstacles before our eyes. These internal obstacles take one of two forms.

We tell ourselves that we lack the ability to do what needs to be done. We don't have the right skills. We don't have the right resources. We don't have the right connections. We don't have the right genetics. Notice how each of these is about us, but they still take on an external feel.

The other potential obstacle is: motivation. We don't want to do what needs to be done. Not really. Sometimes we love the idea of a thing, but we don't want to do the work necessary to get it.

Lack of motivation is a perfectly acceptable reason for not doing something — if we make an intentional decision about it. If we choose not to do something and own that decision, then we're on solid ground. The problem is that a lack of motivation is rarely a conscious decision. Instead, we convince ourselves that it's lack of ability.

This is one of those times we just have to be honest with ourselves.

A Life Designer recognizes the difference between, "I can't" and "I won't."

◆ ◆ ◆

Additional Resources

For more information on identifying, reframing, and working through problems,
check out **What's Your Problem?**
available in the Digital Appendix.

You can access the Digital Appendix here:
www.nevertoolatebook.com

What Are You Afraid Of?

◆◆◆

Behind every "I Can't." Behind every "I Won't." Behind every limiting belief. Behind every obstacle. Behind every default decision, is one thing.

Fear.

Fear of failure. Fear of success. Fear of looking like a fool. Fear of losing everything. Fear of being shunned. Fear of getting too close. Fear of death. Fear of our own greatness. Fear underpins every state of inaction in our lives.

At the same time, fear serves a purpose. Fear keeps us safe. Our Protector uses fear to keep us out of real trouble.

But fear also keeps us down. Fear keeps us in default thinking. Fear keeps us from realizing our full potential.

Our fear isn't going anywhere. It's here to stay. We need to embrace fear. We need to befriend fear. We need to notice what fear is telling us and then decide whether to listen to our fears or to ignore them.

The next four chapters will offer some ways to skillfully work with our fears.

Name Your Fears

◆◆◆

I hate bugs. Anyone who knows me knows that I hate bugs. Pretty much all bugs. Crawling bugs. Flying bugs. You name it, I hate them. And I know I'm not alone.

Why do I hate bugs? They scare me. There. I said it. I'm afraid of bugs.

Afraid of what, exactly? If I see a roach in a restaurant, I'm afraid the place is filthy, and I should be suspicious of my food. Sure. But that's not really what's going on. I'd have the same reaction if I saw one in my house or on the street.

What am I really afraid of? Do I think some little bug is going to beat me in a fight? Do I think they are poisonous? Do I think they're going to crawl into my ear when I'm asleep? No. No. Not really. My fear of bugs is irrational. When I remind myself of this, it helps. Some days, I can actually remove a spider or a centipede from my house peacefully without having to smash them with one of my wife's shoes.

Don't get me wrong, I still hate bugs.

As I write that, it's interesting to feel how much easier it is to say that I hate bugs than it is to say I'm afraid of them. It's because my fear is irrational and if I admit that, I now have to deal with it. It's easier to default to hate, which provides the illusion of control. If I hate something, I'm in control. When I fear something, the thing has control over me.

What are you afraid of? What is holding you back from doing the thing that might change your life for the better?

Can you feel resistance when you think about labeling it as fear? Me too. That's why I hate bugs.

Naming it "fear" is the first step. And ya know what? It's a courageous step.

What are you afraid of?

Make Them
Larger Than Life

◆◆◆

Most fears are somewhat reasonable and rational. That thing that we fear might … really could … happen. If you ask for a raise, your boss might say no. If you have a difficult conversation with your spouse, you might get into a heated argument. If you try to run a marathon, you might discover that it's really, really hard. The consequences are real.

It's just that we tend to exaggerate the potential negative consequences in our subconscious. Your boss might say no, but that probably isn't going to irreversibly damage your reputation. You and your spouse might disagree on that subject, but it doesn't mean your marriage is over. You might discover that running isn't your thing, but it doesn't mean you are doomed to a life of lethargy.

Catastrophizing is one of the techniques that your Protector likes to employ. It will make the consequences extreme so that you don't even try. It hopes you won't try. Your Protector hopes you'll take its word as truth.

Your Protector also knows that if you truly examine your exaggerated fears, they won't hold up under scrutiny.

Give it a try. Take whatever fear you have and ask yourself … *what is the worst thing that could happen if I ask for a raise or introduce myself to that attractive person at the bar?* Odds are, you can come up with something pretty terrible. But then ask yourself, what would happen next? Be sure to make it really bad. What if that thing happened too? Keep pulling the thread. See where it goes. At some point you'll realize the whole thing is an illusion. The real threat, if there even is one, is pretty small compared to the story you've fabricated.

As you play around with your exaggerated fears, you'll realize how they are influencing your decisions and your behavior.

Identify the
Positive Commitment

◆◆◆

What is your relationship to your fear? Does it make you feel guilty? Angry? Disgusted with yourself? Do you wish your fear would just go away? I know I do, sometimes. Our fears are not going away, so we need to change our relationship with them.

If our goal is to work with our fears, even to befriend our fears, we need to look beneath the surface. We know that fear comes from our Protector, but why? What is it trying to accomplish?

Every fear that we hold demonstrates a commitment to something positive in our lives.

I'm afraid to ask for a raise ... because I'm committed to being seen as a team player who doesn't rock the boat.

I'm afraid to ask that attractive person out on a date ... because I'm committed to preserving my own dignity and positive self-image.

I'm afraid to write that novel ... because I am committed to preserving my image as a successful, competent person.

I'm afraid to make adjustments to my diet, even though I know they will be healthier for me ... because I'm committed to enjoying myself and the food that I eat.

Noticing the positive commitments is useful on several levels. For one, it allows us to be a bit more compassionate with ourselves when we experience fear. Guilt and self-loathing are almost always unproductive emotions. Identifying the positive commitment allows us to see our fears in a more positive light.

Noticing the positive commitments that lie beneath our fears also opens the door to new approaches to solving the main problem. How can I ask for a raise in a way that demonstrates my commitment to the team? How can I ask this person on a date in a way that reinforces my dignity and positive self-image? When we ask better questions, we get better answers.

The next chapter talks about how identifying our positive commitment can help us question and test the assumptions that underpin our fear.

Test Your Assumptions

◆◆◆

We love making assumptions. Assumptions are the building blocks of default thinking and they make our lives so much easier. They are so damn convenient. We assume the reason things are the way they are. We assume the answers. We assume what will happen if we do the thing we're thinking about doing. Our assumptive mind is the smartest person we've ever met.

We trust our assumptions, which is convenient because it means we don't have to actually DO anything. This keeps our Protector very, very happy.

What happens when our assumptions run contrary to our deeper goals in life?

Take the fears and positive commitments that we've been working with in the past two chapters. What assumptions might we be making?

I'm afraid to ask for a raise because I'm committed to being seen as a team player who doesn't rock the boat. Are you absolutely certain that your boss will perceive your asking for a raise as rocking the boat? Are you absolutely certain that rocking the boat is a bad thing?

I'm afraid to ask that attractive person out on a date because I'm committed to preserving my own dignity and positive self-image. Are you absolutely certain that the attractive person is going to reject you? Are you certain that if you get rejected it will severely damage your dignity and your self-image?

I'm afraid to make adjustments to my diet, even though I know they will be healthier for me, because I'm committed to enjoying myself and the food that I eat. Are you absolutely certain that eating healthier will mean that you enjoy eating less? If you don't drink alcohol, will your friends shun you? Will you be incapable of having a good time?

The problem with assumptions is they are usually untested. Sometimes there's no evidence whatsoever to support our assumptions. Sometimes there is evidence, but it's old and likely outdated. It's just like that elephant with his chains. You should test them every once in a while.

We'll talk more about this in a later chapter: *Experiments, Prototypes, and The Little Things.*

Additional Resources

For more information about identifying and working with your fears,
check out **What Are You So Afraid Of?**
available in the Digital Appendix.

You can access the Digital Appendix here:
www.nevertoolatebook.com

How Do I Get There?

◆◆◆

A weary traveler is trying to get across a raging creek. He happens upon a farmer working his field and asks if there's an easy way to get to the other side of the creek. The farmer says, "Yeah, sure. You just want to go back downstream about a mile, then..." He pauses. "No, you're better off going upstream, about a half-mile..." Again, the farmer pauses. "Come to think of it. You can't get there from here."

This is how it often feels with Life Design. Come to think of it, this is how it usually feels. We have a good sense of where we need to go. Sometimes we can even see it from where we're standing. Yet it feels like there's no way to get there, from here.

Now that you've determined where you are, where you want to go, and what's stopping you, it's time to focus on getting from here to there. That's what the next few chapters are all about. We're going to identify the people you'll want to have on your Life Design team and how to enroll them in your project. We're going to talk about how to develop an approach that helps you move in the right direction and make sure you stay on the right path.

Are you ready to get across this creek?

Don't Go Solo

◆◆◆

In the early stages we're tempted to keep our Life Design a secret. It feels risky to tell people that we want to change our life. It means revealing that we're are not perfectly happy, which makes us feel vulnerable. Even worse, if we share our ideas, the other person may laugh at us or tell us we're crazy. *I know I'm crazy. I don't need you telling me that. Geez.* Of course, some of us are just too proud to ask for help from anyone.

When it comes to Life Design, there are two reasons that isolation is a bad idea.

First, our work absolutely will impact the people around us. It's inevitable. When we make changes to one part of our life, it affects other areas, including our relationships.

On top of that, Life Design changes us. As we become more intentional, more aware, more accountable and more empowered, others will notice. Each person will have a unique reaction. Some will be curious. Some will be supportive. Many will feel threatened.

Why would anyone feel threatened? It's our work. It's our life. Right?

Not exactly. The people around us are probably comfortable with us just the way we are. Most people are living by default, and a consistent version of "you" is part of that reality. Plus, seeing us make changes to our lives forces the other person to grapple with their life. Life By Default only works when everyone does it. If one person questions the system, the whole thing comes down.

The second reason we shouldn't go solo when it comes to Life Design is that we are going to need help. It doesn't matter how determined or how capable we are, we'll get further and move faster if we have help from others. We'll benefit from their experiences, their expertise, and their outside perspectives. We'll also use other people as a source of energy, motivation and support.

Life Designers know that it's a collaborative process.

Over the next few chapters, we'll explore some of the collaborative structures you may want to use in your Life Design work.

Your Design Team

◆◆◆

" Great things in business are never
done by one person;
they're done by a team of people.

– Steve Jobs

The sooner we start to think of our Life Design as a team effort, the sooner we will make real progress. And I'm not talking about conceptually or metaphorically. I'm talking literally. A team. A design team. Uniforms and all.

Membership to our design team isn't a lifetime appointment. Our team should change based on the types of projects that we're working on. (More about projects in a few chapters.) We select members of our team based on the knowledge, skills, and energy they bring. This is where a bit of self-awareness comes in handy. We don't want our design team to consist of people who look and think like us. We need diversity because diversity overcomes complexity. We need to find people who complement us. (Not to be confused with people who compliment us.)

How big does our team need to be? Of course, it depends on the size of the project the team is trying to tackle. But probably no less than three people and no more than seven. Too few people means our team will lack horsepower and too many people will make our team unwieldy.

As we design our team, we should consider what makes for an effective team:

- Team members are carefully chosen because they bring something necessary to the team.

- Team members know they are part of the team.

- Team members know their role and unique contribution.

- Team members have clear assignments and they understand the importance of their job.

As you make the shift from thinking about your Life Design as a solo project into thinking about having formal team at your back, you'll experience a surge of courage and confidence. It's also nice to know that we don't have to do all of the work ourselves. The pressure drops and we begin to see the challenge as a fun, collaborative effort.

Life Designers always design a team around them.

Additional Resources

Check out the **Life Design Team** worksheet, available in the Digital Appendix.

You can access the Digital Appendix here:
www.nevertoolatebook.com

Coaches and Mentors

◆◆◆

"Our chief want in life is somebody
who will make us do what we can.
- Ralph Waldo Emerson

There will be days when it feels like all hope is lost. There will be stretches when nothing goes right and we begin to question everything. *Why bother? What is the point if nothing ever changes? Maybe I'm not cut out for this?* These questions mark the arrival of the "dog days."

The dog days usually come in the middle of the project. Our initial energy and enthusiasm have tapered off. We've probably made a few changes to our life already, so everything feels disrupted and unstable. Perhaps even chaotic. We may feel like it's too late to turn back, but too scary to move forward. Panic sets in. We freak out.

In these moments, we need stability. We need a reassuring voice. Someone to remind us why we set out on this path and to convince us that we have what it takes to continue. We need a helping hand. We need a kick in the butt.

Our coach, or our mentor, is the most critical member of our design team. They are always there, with a kind word, or to challenge our assumptions. They give us affirmation and validation, but also call us out when we need it. We cherish their perspective and their persistent belief that we are worthy of our own greatness.

If you don't already have a coach or a mentor, get one.

The Perfect Plan

◆◆◆

I remember my first marathon. At the time the idea of running 26.2 miles felt absurd, but a group of my friends were pretty set on the idea. I've always been a terrible runner. My college lacrosse coach once described my gait as "glacial." How could I possibly pull off a marathon? I started doing some research.

It turns out, marathon training is pretty simple. That's not to say it's easy, but the formula is simple. There are programs that guide you through the entire training process. It's simply a matter of running the recommended mileage each day. Start off with shorter runs and gradually work up to long runs, and then taper off in the weeks right before the race. Very straightforward.

The plan made a huge thing feel manageable. The idea of running 26.2 miles was daunting, but the idea of running 4 miles a few times in a week was doable. The next week I had to run 6 miles. And so on, and so on, until the finish line.

Life Design is similar in that it feels daunting to think about our life as a whole and thinking about making a major change isn't any better. We need to break things down. We need to be intentional. We need a plan.

The plan doesn't need to be perfect. It won't be.

For the remainder of Book Two we're going to explore some of the elements and options available to you as you develop your Life Design plan.

Experiments, Prototypes, and the Little Things

◆◆◆

"I have not failed. I've just found
10,000 ways that won't work

- Thomas Edison

For as long as there have been people, there have been ideas and there have been failures. The notion that our failures have something valuable to tell us has been around just as long. From Confucius to Colin Powell, big thinkers have noticed that failure isn't really failing, it's learning.

And yet...

Failing still sucks.

Nobody likes to fail. Even if we know that failure is inevitable, that failure is the price of admission, we still try to avoid it at all costs. Michael Jordan can tell us all day long about the shots that he missed during the big moments. It doesn't help. He's still Michael Jordan and he's still got 6 championship rings. It's tough to make the connection between failure and greatness. But unless we do, we won't be willing to put ourselves out there, where we might miss and, even worse, where we might be judged.

We have to change our relationship with failure, and a quote on a coffee mug isn't going to get the job done. We need a process. We need a mental model that actually works. Luckily, scientists, product designers, and Japanese automakers have figured it out.

Scientists don't stumble into discoveries. They experiment their way into them. The scientist starts with an idea, a hypothesis, and they design an experiment to test it. The scientist doesn't have expectations that an experiment will "work." Scientists don't think like that. The results of the experiment either support or disprove the hypothesis, or the experiment is inconclusive. A successful experiment isn't one that proves the hypothesis. A successful experiment is one that isn't corrupted by a flawed approach, or by outside factors. The integrity of the process paramount, the results are an interesting byproduct.

How does a sexy product, like the iPhone or a Tesla, come into existence? Does the idea just pop into some product designer's head and … voila! Nope. Not even close. The road from concept to final product is a long one. Product designers know their first idea is not the right idea. They know even their best ideas will fall apart as soon as they start sharing them with *real* people. Instead, the designers create prototypes. A prototype is a scaled-down model. The prototype doesn't have all the bells and whistles the end product will probably have, but is close enough for now. The prototype doesn't need to be perfect. It only needs to be good enough for the designers to learn *something* when they hand the prototype to a potential customer. The best prototypes yield a lot of useful information within minimal cost.

That brings us to the Japanese automakers and the concept of "Kaizen." The term became popular in the 1980s, when the Japanese were dominating the U.S. auto market and much of their success was attributed to the concept of Kaizen. Kaizen is often translated as "continuous improvement," but the real beauty of Kaizen lies beneath the surface. Kaizen is not about making big changes. With Kaizen, even the smallest change is valuable, as long as it's in the right direction. Small changes lead to big changes. No change is too small as long as it is a positive change. In fact, the smaller the change, the better, because it's more likely to stick.

How does all of this translate to Life Design?

A good Life Designer uses experiments to test their ideas. As we conduct our experiments, we are less concerned about the outcome of the experiment and more interested in the quality and integrity of our approach. Discovery is the desired outcome.

Life Designers don't make massive, irreversible changes. We don't put all of our eggs in one fancy, over-engineered, basket. We use scaled-down models to test our ideas in the real world. With the feedback we receive, we'll develop the confidence to make bigger and bigger changes to our Life Design.

A Life Designer realizes that no change is too small as long as it moves us in the right direction. The smaller, the better.

Additional Resources

Check out the **Kaizen** worksheet, available in the Digital Appendix.

You can access the Digital Appendix here:
www.nevertoolatebook.com

Curious Conversations

◆◆◆

What if your goal is to take your career in a new direction? You can't just quit your job and hope that you find your way into a great new career that lights your heart on fire and also has a great healthcare plan. Right?

Of course not. That would be a bad design with a high risk of catastrophic failure. So how do we design an experiment or build a prototype to simulate a new career?

I'm about to share with you a lesson that I wish I had learned in my 20s. Hell, I wish I learned it in my teens. I call it **curious conversations**.

Whatever our Life Design goals may be, chances are there is someone nearby who has done it, is doing it, or already has it in their life. Even if their story isn't exactly the same as ours, we'll get a lot from talking to them. There's nothing better than hearing from someone who's been there, done that. Keep in mind, we're not talking about entering into a long-term coaching or mentoring relationship here. We're talking about a conversation. We're talking coffee.

Why would someone want to talk to us? It's simple. We'll be talking to them about their favorite topic in the whole world: themselves. Everyone likes to talk about themselves. It's incredibly validating. As soon as we let the person know that we're only interested in hearing their story, they will find the time. As long as they know we're not going to pitch them a set of steak knives or ask them to read our latest manuscript, they'll be happy to talk. They'll be flattered. Setting up the conversation might go something like this...

Hey Jane, I've always admired XYZ about you and I wonder if you might be willing to tell me your story of how you got XYZ. If you can spare 30 minutes, I'll buy lunch, coffee, or a beer.

If we are intentional and we plan ahead, we'll get more value from those 30 minutes than from a year of experimentation, a weekend seminar, or any book. (This one notwithstanding.)

Curious conversations are a strategy. A tactic. They don't just happen. Life Designers make them happen.

Designing Projects

◆ ◆ ◆

What is a project? At the most basic level, a project is a logical grouping of work, aimed at achieving a specific outcome. Projects make the work feel less daunting. Projects help us strategize our approach and see how all of the parts fit together. Thanks to their structure, projects help to keep us on track.

Suppose, for example, our Life Design ambition is to "get healthier." This isn't a project. It's more of a theme. We might design one or more projects to move us in the direction of the theme. For example, some complementary projects could be:

Lose 20 pounds.

Or…

Complete a Tough Mudder adventure race.

Feel the difference?

A project has a specific outcome. It should be obvious when our project is complete. There should be a finish line. Literally, or figuratively. Your project may not have a shiny medal at the end of it, but it should be just as tangible.

A project is big enough that it's going to take some time to complete, but not so much time that we lose sight of the end goal. Usually 3-6 months is a nice duration for a project.

A project should be complex enough that we can break it down into smaller components that fit together to make a larger whole. For example, a weight loss plan or a Tough Mudder training plan might prescribed exercise, such as walking, running or swimming. These activities could be broken down into weekly and daily mileage targets. This detailed structure allowed us to ask the questions *Did I do what I was supposed to do today? Did I accomplish my goal for the week?*

The beauty of a project structure is that it allows us to monitor our progress through a series of smaller goals. If we find that we're missing our daily goals or coming up short of our weekly mileage week after week, we know that our project is off schedule, and we can make the necessary adjustments.

Where does the project come from? From the work we've already done, of course. Go back to the work that you did in these chapters: *A Quick Assessment, More or Less, But Why? and Identify Themes, Not Goals.* Each of these should provide you with solid ideas for what to include in your project. You may want to incorporate some of your inner journey work into your project too, but don't feel the need to force that in the early stages.

The project emerges when you identify a desired outcome. *I want to hike the Appalachian Trail. I want to publish my first novel. I want to generate 20k of supplemental annual income through real estate investments.* What is it that you want to accomplish by the end of the project?

When it comes to designing projects much of the value is in the design process. For me, the act of identifying a big goal and breaking it down into smaller parts is both insightful and therapeutic. If I can't describe the steps required to accomplish something, then I don't really understand what I'm doing and I'm not likely to do it well.

Thinking about life in terms of projects is new for many of us. It takes some practice to become comfortable with the idea. Luckily, we've got time.

Life Designers are patient project managers.

Additional Resources

Check out the **Projects, Practices, and Habits Overview** worksheet, available in the Digital Appendix.

You can access the Digital Appendix here:
www.nevertoolatebook.com

Designing Practices

◆ ◆ ◆

Practices are one of the most useful tools in the Life Designer's kit. They are also incredibly underused and misunderstood. Most of us would say that we practice things all the time. But there's a difference between "practices" and "practicing."

Practicing is about developing skills.

Practices are about cultivating a state of mind.

It can be confusing because practicing and practices can look quite similar. Both involve doing a specific activity over and over. Both develop skills and competency. Both require an investment of time and energy, and in both cases, what you get out of it depends on what you put in. Also, both are useful when it comes to Life Design.

Okay, so what's the difference?

Here's an example … I practice writing every day. I read books about writing. I solicit feedback from other people about my writing. I work with Robyn, my editor. I read my own writing with a critical eye. I do these things to become a better writer.

I also have a **writing practice**. Every morning, before I open my email, before I look at my to-do list, before I do anything, I write. Usually free-hand, with my favorite pen. My goal is 20 minutes, but I can go anywhere from a minute to an hour. Never less than a minute, though. I'm not allowed to skip the practice entirely. I can do one minute if that's what my body tells me is the right amount, but I can't do zero.

Does my writing practice make me a better writer? Sure. But that is not the point. I believe my writing practice makes me a better person.

When I was training for my first marathon, I practiced running every day. I followed my plan. I made adjustments to my pacing and to my form. I practiced running, but I didn't have a running practice. I wasn't looking for running to play a bigger role in my life. I know a lot of people who use a running practice to cultivate a desired state of mind. It all comes down to our personal objectives.

Life Designers practice when practice is needed, but the thing that separates Life Designers from the rest are their practices.

◆ ◆ ◆

Additional Resources

Check out the **Designing Practices** worksheet, available in the Digital Appendix.

You can access the Digital Appendix here:
www.nevertoolatebook.com

Designing Habits

◆◆◆

We all have habits. Things we do every day, without thought. Many of our habits formed out of default thinking. At some point we just started doing something, nothing bad happened, so we kept doing it. Life Designers eliminate the habits that were born from default thinking and replace them with intentionally designed habits. Let me show you what I mean…

I've gotten into the habit of using my smartphone as my alarm clock. Every night, I sleep with my phone right next to my bed. If I wake up in the middle of the night, I often check the time on my phone. It's the first thing I see when I wake up in the morning. Since my phone is right there, I usually check my emails before I even get out of bed. (Yeah, I know, I'm supposed to do my writing practice first.) On my worst days, I even browse one or more of my social media accounts. What started off as convenience has evolved into one of my worst habits.

I doubt there is a worse way for someone to begin their day. I need to break myself of this habit because I find my attention and focus are much better when I write first thing in the morning. I'm more creative. I'm more energized. I'm funnier. I suspect I'm better-looking.

I need to develop some more effective, less tech-focused morning habits.

Habits are like a moving sidewalk — once we step on, the machine does the work for us. The thing about moving sidewalks is we don't have any choice where it brings us. The destination is predetermined. Once we establish a habit and then trigger it, the rest just happens. Habits require very little thought. This is both the power of habit and the curse.

Whether a habit is beneficial or detrimental is usually a function of how we formed the habit in the first place. Intentional, well-designed habits usually move us in the right direction. Brushing our teeth, for example. Habits that happen by default usually have terrible consequences. Grabbing a candy bar at the checkout line comes to mind.

Another nice feature of habits is that we can string them together to accomplish a complex result. Author S.J. Scott calls this "habit stacking" in his book by the same name.

I've created a habit stack that works well for me in the area of my physical health. Each night before bed, I put my workout clothes into my gym bag, along with my Kindle and my headphones. I then put the bag next to the back door where I'll see it as I head out the next morning and this helps me remember to put the bag on the passenger seat of my car. When I get back into the car after work my bag is right there, as a reminder to swing by the gym on the way home. Since I'm always reading or listening to an audiobook, I've got my Kindle and headphones right there with me as well. The whole system just works, and as a result of this habit stack, I exercise far more consistently than I would without it.

I find that habits are incredibly low maintenance. I rarely, if ever, outgrow them. As long as they are pointing me in a positive direction, I just let them run their course. Build the moving sidewalk that leads you toward where you want to go, and then ride that sucker every day.

Life Designers recognize the power of habits and design habits that support their overall Life Design goals.

Additional Resources

Check out the **Designing Habits** worksheet, available in the Digital Appendix.

You can access the Digital Appendix here: www.nevertoolatebook.com

Designing Disturbances

◆◆◆

*"*We choose to go to the moon in this decade

and do the other things,

not because they are easy, but because they are hard…

- John F. Kennedy

In the Introduction to this book I described my vision quest experience from 2014. This was an example of something I call a **designed disturbance**. A design disturbance is an intentionally disruptive and challenging situation undertaken with the goal of opening the space for great epiphany and discovery.

Rarely do we have epiphanies and discoveries when we are operating from our comfort zone. In fact, our Protector doesn't want us to have these experiences because it knows that as soon as we have one, our life will change forever. As you know, our Protector would much prefer we stay on the couch, where nothing can hurt us.

What does it take to design a disturbance?

A designed disturbance involves total immersion. It's best if there is little or no chance to escape. I'm not suggesting we put ourself in grave danger, but if we can simply stop the experience as soon as it gets uncomfortable, it defeats the purpose. The power of a designed disturbance is in the struggle. In the case of my vision quest, I was deep in the wilderness, surrounded by nature and far from anyone who could help me, or distract me. I could have walked out at any time, but it would have required work. It would have required admitting defeat.

The best designed disturbances involve the body as well as the mind. Something magical happens when we move our body, when we are forced to overcome some physical discomfort. When we engage multiple systems simultaneously. I could have taken a tent, an air mattress, and five days' worth of gourmet meals with me on my vision quest. But I didn't.

To get the most out of our designed disturbance, we must be fully present. Nobody likes being uncomfortable. Our minds, if not our bodies, will desperately try to escape. I don't know how many hours I spent thinking about hamburgers while I sat on my rock in the woods. Though my mind tried to wander, there was only so far it could go without the aid of my smart phone, or a book, or my family and friends to take me away. When we're engaged in a designed disturbance, we are doing real work, so we should honor it with the fullest attention and intention that we can muster.

Of course, not everyone can drop everything to head off on a five-day vision quest. No problem. There are a lot of ways to have a full-body, fully present, immersive experience.

Take up a martial art.

Go to a foreign country where you don't speak the language, but learn to get by.

Learn to play an instrument.

Do an adventure race.

Go on a blind date.

Sing karaoke in a bar full of strangers.

Volunteer at a soup kitchen.

Remember, these are just ideas. When designing disturbances, we must calibrate them to our own tolerance levels. What qualifies as a disturbance for us might not register a blip on someone else's radar, and vice versa.

Look again at the list of ideas above. Disregard the one you already think you could probably do. Consider the one that scares the crap out of you. The one that makes you deeply uncomfortable at the mere thought of attempting it.

Now keep that level of outside-your-comfort-zone challenge in mind, and design a disturbance for yourself.

How Do You Measure Up?

◆◆◆

"What gets measured, gets done." This is an old saying in business and I've found it to be true. When I served as the Chief Operating Officer for a consulting firm with 200 employees, we relied heavily on this principle.

There was a stretch of time when we noticed our expenses were getting a little out of hand and it was contributing to a decline in profits. Specifically, we noticed executives were charging expensive flights and meals to the company more and more often. We created a report that highlighted executives who turned in excessive expenses on our monthly conference call. After the second month we noticed a positive change in behavior.

Was it because executives didn't like having attention called to their questionable spending habits in front of their peers? Was it because the act of measuring the behavior caused execs to be more cognizant of their spending? I suspect it was a little of both.

If we want to make change happen, we need to design a system for measuring our progress toward our goals.

Don't worry, we're not talking about creating a complex project management tracking system. We're talking about simple ways to keep tabs on what we are doing, how often we are doing it, and what kind of results we are getting.

Why is measurement so important? The next few chapters will make the case for measurement.

Measurement
Raises Awareness

◆◆◆

I generally keep an eye on my weight, but every now and again I'll find that I've put on a few extra pounds. It usually correlates to the holiday season, or the summer, or stretches of days that end with "y." Whenever I find myself slipping into some bad eating habits or falling out of my exercise routine, I use two simple techniques to help get myself back on track.

Habit #1: I weigh myself every morning. I put my digital scale right in front of my shower to remind me to weigh myself as soon as I wake up. The idea of weighing yourself every morning isn't new. I've known about it for years, but it wasn't until I became intentional about weighing myself daily that I appreciated the benefits.

For me, the main benefit isn't monitoring progress. I don't get a lot of benefit in comparing one day to the next because my weight fluctuates so much day-to-day. The benefit for me is that I increase my attention and my attunement to my body and my goals for eating well and losing weight. Stepping on the scale is a reminder of how I want to behave throughout the day.

Habit #2: I track my calories for three weeks. I use a simple app on my phone that allows me to log the foods that I eat. I find that three weeks is enough time for me to get a general sense of what types of food I'm eating and how many calories and macronutrients I'm taking in. Monitoring my calorie intake daily gives me a real sense of the choices that I make and how they impact my overall diet. At one point I realized that I could make one (and only one) bad eating choice each day and still hit my target calorie intake, as long as I worked out for 30 minutes.

Again, the goal of this detailed tracking isn't to micromanage every decision I make. Rather, by paying close attention to my eating for about three weeks I'm able to raise my awareness enough that I can go 6-8 months without having to worry about going off the rails. As my eating habits change, I'll reinstitute the practice for another three weeks until my awareness is sufficiently raised again.

Life By Design is about recognizing the moments of decision in our lives and then making conscious choices. Through measurement, we raise our awareness, which allows us to recognize those moments as they arise.

Measurement
Fosters Accountability

◆◆◆

I remember a few years back when the Fitbit first came on the scene and people were sharing their step-count results with friends. That was a powerful accountability mechanism. Measurement makes shared accountability easier and more effective.

If you've ever worked with a personal trainer then you know the transformative power of accountability. You've probably noticed the difference between groups where shared accountability is high and groups where it's not. When shared accountability is high, people show up. People do the work. When shared accountability is lacking, personal motivation is also often lacking.

Life Designers recognize that willpower only goes so far. By creating measurement mechanisms that allow other people to participate in our Life Design process, we gain the power of shared accountability.

Measurement
Increases Motivation

I love winning. Who doesn't? Winning, even small victories, lets us know that we're capable. Winning lets us know we're on the right track. We're making progress.

You can't win without keeping score.

Devise your measurement. Do the work. Hit your targets. And celebrate your mini victories.

Measurement
Helps You Calibrate

◆◆◆

Back in the old days (before GPS) it was possible to get really, really lost. Nowadays, our smart phone tells us immediately that we're off track. "Proceed to the route. Proceed to the route." *I know! I know!*

The nice thing about measuring is we can tell if we are actually making progress or just spinning our wheels. And we can make adjustments as necessary. In the early days of my business, my sales were lacking. I was doing lots of activities that I thought were valuable. I was busy. Working hard. But the numbers couldn't lie. The revenue wasn't there.

What happens if we find that we are consistently missing our milestones? It could be that our approach is not working, and we need to rethink our plan. In my case, I realized that I was busy, but busy with the wrong tasks. I needed to adjust my approach and create a new measurement system to ensure that I was following the new approach. That meant making more sales calls and spending less time on secondary activities, such as developing my website and business cards. Instead of measuring how many hours I worked each day, I started measuring how many sales calls I made each day. Sure enough, it wasn't long before I began seeing my revenue numbers moving in the right direction.

A Life Designer uses measurement to identify areas where fine-tuning adjustments may be necessary in order to achieve the overall plan.

Additional Resources

Check out the **Projects, Practices, and Habits** worksheet for some ideas about how to implement measurement into your Life Design.

You can access the Digital Appendix here: www.nevertoolatebook.com

A Change of Plans

◆◆◆

"Everyone has a plan
until they get punched in the face.

- Mike Tyson

Life punches us all in the face every now and again. When it does, we change our plans. We may find that we didn't understand how things really worked, until we got into the thick of it, and we realize our approach won't work. Sometimes we discover new information that renders our original plan invalid. Sometimes we change our mind about what we want. When any of these happen, we may need to change our plan.

Wait, we're allowed to change the plan?

Sure. It would be foolish to assume that once we choose a direction, we have to continue in that direction indefinitely. The beauty of treating our Life Design as a series of experiments is that when things don't work out the way we expected or hoped, we can change direction.

Over the course of your Life Design journey, you will probably find yourself having strayed from your original plan. When this happens, don't beat yourself up, because it happens to all of us. Straying from our plan usually means one of two things. It might be an indication that our plan wasn't optimal for us. Perhaps it was too aggressive. Perhaps it was simply on the wrong track. It does happen. Before disregarding the plan entirely, we should consider an alternate explanation.

It's possible that our original plan was sound, but that we simply needed a break. Personal development work can be exhausting and we all need a break from time to time to allow our mind, body, and spirit to recharge and to allow any new learnings to settle and stabilize. In a perfect world we would notice that we need a break and we would be intentional about taking one. But this isn't a perfect world. When we do find ourselves straying from a good plan, we just need to thank our intuition for giving us a break. And then gently move back to the plan.

It can be tricky to tell the difference between a flawed plan and needing to take a short break. Unfortunately, there is no easy solution to this problem. If we find ourselves continuously staying from the plan, particularly before we make any real progress, it probably means the plan is flawed and we need to go deeper to understand why we can't stick to it.

In the end, it's up to us to decide if we need to push through or if we need to revise our plan. With practice and observation, we'll get better at recognizing our patterns and tendencies when it comes to pushing through or changing directions.

Life Designers are intentional when it comes to changing their plan.

At the Threshold

◆ ◆ ◆

Congratulations, again! You've reached another milestone in the Life Design journey. How are you feeling? Excited? Challenged? Perhaps a bit overwhelmed? Maybe a bit scared?

Good. I'd be worried if you weren't.

The apprehension that you're feeling is your Protector, doing its thing. It's probably been using all of the usual arguments against you so far. But your Protector saved the most powerful for last. This is the one that really gets me fired up, because this an out-and-out lie. Your Protector says...

It's too late.

You know what I say to that? Nope. It's not too late. It's never too late.

I know it's not too late because your Protector is talking, and it only feels the need to speak when something is actually possible. Your Protector doesn't bother with warnings or arguments when something is impossible. For example, I'm never going to marry Angelina Jolie, despite my deep and pitiful longing. I know this. My Protector knows this and is perfectly happy to let me hang onto the dream because it knows I'll never do anything about it. My Protector doesn't need to talk me out of my illusion. It won't waste the breath.

Your Protector knows what you know. It's not too late. It's possible and you both know it. All that remains is to step through that next door.

BOOK THREE

—

The Reward

The Ultimate Questions

◆◆◆

What are my gifts? Who are my people?

In the end, these are the questions that every Life Designer is seeking to answer. All of the hard work. The inevitable setbacks. The growing pains. All in service to answering these two questions.

Heck, let's make it even simpler. One question.

What do I have to offer the world?

When you overcome default thinking and begin to Live By Design, you are no longer playing the same game as the rest of the people. You don't have all of the answers. Nobody does. You are not immune to pain or to fear, but you recognize that pain and fear serve important purposes in our lives and you know how to work with them. You are not free from struggle. Everyone struggles. As a Life Designer, you recognize the struggle is The Work.

You have so much to offer.

Go serve. Go do your work.

Make Inertia Your Friend

◆◆◆

An object at rest will remain at rest until an outside force acts upon it. This is the essence of default thinking. If you do nothing, life will remain as it is today. Things don't usually get better by chance.

Do you recognize that first sentence? It's Newton's Law of Inertia. If you can remember all the way back to elementary school, then you know there is second part: An object in motion will remain in motion until an outside force acts upon it.

When you are stuck in default thinking, inertia is your enemy. But when you are in motion, inertia is your friend.

Life Design is about getting into motion.

Regretfully Yours

◆◆◆

When I was five, my sister and her husband took me to Orlando for two weeks. One of my favorite parts of that trip was our visit to an amusement park, fun house. In fact, my sister was shocked when she asked me what I wanted to do on our last day and I requested a return visit to the fun house. So much for Disney World.

After four decades, that fun house remains one of my most vivid regrets in life.

My brother-in-law, Lou, and I stood before two doors. One normal-sized and one tiny, as if made for a little tyke like me. Lou dropped down to his knees and made for the small door. I stopped him, pointing toward the big door.

"But we went that way last time," Lou said. "Let's go through this one."

"No." I insisted we go through the big door. Maybe I was scared of that small space. Maybe I knew that I had a good time going through the big door and didn't want to gamble on the unknown. All I know is that Lou let me choose, and I chose the big door — again.

I still wonder what I missed.

People think the antidote to regret is action. It's not. The antidote to regret is *intention*.

I knew back then I should choose the tiny door and I still chose the big one. I opted for safe. I regretted it the second I made the decision to default to my comfort zone.

The Choice

◆◆◆

Kara watches as her husband cuts an inch off each end of the pot roast and tosses the ends into the trash. Confused, she asks, "Why did throw away perfectly good meat?"

"That's how I was taught to cook pot roast," Steve replies. "It's how my mom did it and it's how I've always done it."

Kara presses Steve until he agrees to call his mother and ask why she taught him to make pot roast this way. So he calls.

"It turns out, mom used to cut the ends off because her pan was too short to hold a full roast."

All those years of wasted beef! Why hadn't Steve ever questioned the strange practice? Simple: Default thinking. *This is the way things are so this is the way things must be.* Although Steve was throwing away the ends of the roast all those years, he never actually "chose" to do it. Choosing requires thought. Choosing requires intention.

Life Design is about making choices. Life Design is being intentional about what you include and what you exclude from your life. Life Design is taking an honest assessment of where you are right now and where you think you want to be, and then doing something to close the gap. Life Design is about taking action and owning the results.

Life Design is about showing up every day with total authenticity and a commitment to becoming the best version of you possible. Do that every day and you won't regret it.

There is No Tomorrow

◆ ◆ ◆

"The best day to plant a tree is yesterday.
The second best is today.
- Chinese proverb

Procrastination is a weapon of default-thinking.

Procrastination is the enemy.

The enemy deserves no mercy.

There is no tomorrow.

It's never too late because we always have today.

Start Today.

Painting Bridges

♦♦♦

There's an urban legend that says, the job of painting the Golden Gate Bridge is never finished. As soon as they finish painting, the workers go right back to the beginning and start over. Though it doesn't quite work like that, it's generally true. Workers are always painting some part of the massive bridge. It is a continuous work in progress.

The Work of Life Design is never finished. We are each a work in progress. There is always something that warrants attention, even if it's just routine maintenance. Keep your brushes handy. And be sure to take some time every so often to step back and admire the view.

It's a beautiful bridge.

The End.

What's Next?

◆◆◆

I mentioned all the way back in the very first chapter, *Never Too Late* is an invitation.

Throughout the process of writing this book I struggled with the decision about how much to put in and how much to leave out. Should I put in a ton of real-life examples from past clients? Should I put in a bunch of references to research and pull in similar ideas by other industry experts?

I decided to write a book that I would want to read. These days my attention span is short. I want to get to the point, quickly. I want to be inspired by great ideas. If there's something that intrigues me, that I want to know more about, I will go find it. If there's not, I can walk away without having invested too much of my time or my money.

That was my approach and I hope it worked for you.

What if you want more? What if *Never Too Late* left you with more questions than answers? To some extent, that was the goal. After all, there is only so much you can do with a book. If a book causes me to ask important questions, it was worthwhile.

I've thrown a lot at you in these pages. There are literally dozens of concepts and techniques. There's no way you could have a full appreciation for all of them. My recommendation is to go back and review one or two of the concepts again, allowing yourself to really take them in. Download the corresponding worksheets and start trying to apply the concepts to your life.

Which concepts should you choose? I have two thoughts on this. First, you can choose a concept that really spoke to you. Something that you feel applies to your life right now. If you can sense an immediate application to your life, that's likely a good place to start.

Alternatively, if there was a chapter that felt really foreign, that didn't resonate with you at all, that might be a good place to start. Sometimes the thing that we resist is the thing that we need most.

I've written N2L in a way that invites you to go back to specific chapters, over and over again. I'm hoping its the kind of book you pick up anytime you feel lost, stuck, or find yourself longing for something else in your life.

The Invitation

I recognize that for some people, reading this book will feel like a starter's gun, and they'll be off to the races, making changes to their life right away. But I suspect most people will want to learn more. There are a few options to do that, which I'll share with you here. A few of them are free and a few of them cost money. I want to be clear; this is how I make my living and, frankly, selling books doesn't pay the bills! That said, I hate most of the sleazy sales pitches that come into my inbox every hour. If you decide you want to purchase something from the Life Design Center, I want to make that as risk-free of a decision as you'll ever make. So, here is my invitation:

Never Too Late Online Course - This is a stand-alone online course that dives deeper into the principles that I introduce in the book. The course is self-paced and is delivered primarily in video format. If you've ever seen Masterclass, it feels a lot like those. There's also a monthly live call that you are welcome to join anytime you like as well as a private discussion group. The normal cost of the online course is $99 for lifetime access. However, if you've purchased the book, the course is only $49. I encourage people to purchase and read the book first, so they can decide if the course is right for them. You can get your discount coupon in the Digital Appendix at:

www.nevertoolatebook.com

Never Too Late Masterclass - This is a 12-week (online) program that includes live group calls, offline video trainings, interactive discussions, and small group work. The Masterclass will go even deeper into the core topics from the book, but with the benefits of live instruction, from me, as well as interaction with your fellow classmates. This is a high-energy class that will really get you fired up while holding you accountable. I recognize the most people don't do well in a purely online, self-paced learning environment, so the Masterclass is great for them. Pricing for the Masterclass is available in the Digital Appendix. Once again, we offer a significant discount for anyone who has purchased the book and/or the online course.

Intentional Tuesdays (Free) - This is my weekly blog/vlog where we cover all kinds of Life Design topics. I also offer exclusive content and occasional bonus materials to subscribers. You can check out the blog or subscribe here:

www.lifedesigncenter.com/intentionaltuesdays

Start Your Own Mastermind Group - Maybe you are not ready to name your full design team, but that doesn't mean you shouldn't start collaborating right now. Do you know a few other people who might have a thing or two they'd like to work on in their lives? One of the best ways to build some early momentum is to start a *mastermind group*. If you are not familiar with the concept, think of it as a book club, on steroids. Get a group of 3-7 people and set up a regular study group. Perhaps you'll meet weekly or every other week to discuss core concepts from the book. Mastermind groups are a great way to enhance learning through shared experience and they are also tremendous for building safe accountability structures. From the Digital Appendix, you can download a free *Never Too Late Mastermind Workbook* that will walk you through the process of setting up and running your very own mastermind group. It's not nearly as hard as you might be thinking!

—

There you have it. That's my invitation. I hope to see you soon.
Prosperous Journey,
-zog

Made in the
USA
Monee, IL